D0578154

Favorite Psalms

Selected and expounded by

John Stott

MOODY PRESS

Copyright © 1988 Three's Company
Text © 1988 John Stott
Photographs © 1988 Three's
Company

All rights reserved. No part of this
publication may be reproduced, or
transmitted in any form or by any
means, electronic or mechanical,
including photocopy, recording, or
any information storage and retrieval
system, without permission in writing
from the publisher.

Scripture quotations in this
publication are from the *Holy Bible,
New International Version.*
Copyright © 1973, 1978, 1984 by
the International Bible Society.
Published in the U.K. by Hodder &
Stoughton.

Designed and created by
Three's Company
12 Flitcroft Street
London WC2H 8DJ

Worldwide co-edition organised and
produced by Angus Hudson Ltd
Greater London House
Hampstead Road
London NW1 7QX

Design: Peter M.Wyart MSIAD
Editor: Tim Dowley

Typesetting by Watermark

Printed in Great Britain by
Purnell Book Production Ltd
Paulton

British Commonwealth edition
published by
Word Publishing
Word (UK) Ltd
Milton Keynes
England

ISBN 0–85009–158–6

First published in the USA by
Moody Press
820 N. LaSalle Drive
Chicago, Il 60610
USA
2nd printing, 1989

ISBN 0–8024–4770–8

Moody Press, a ministry of the
Moody Bible Institute, is designed for
education, evangelization, and
edification. If we may assist you in
knowing more about Christ and the
Christian life, please write us without
obligation:
Moody Press, c/o MLM,
Chicago, Illinois 60610
USA

Published in Canada by
RG Mitchell Family Books Inc.
565 Gordon Baker Road
Willowdale, Ontario
Canada M2H 2W2

ISBN 0–9693201–5–9

Contents

Preface

It would be impossible to stop Christians singing. One of the sure signs of the fullness of the Holy Spirit is to "sing and make music in your heart to the Lord" (Ephesians 5:18,19). Especially when we come together to worship, our praises would be inconceivable without songs. So we say to one another, "Come, let us sing for joy to the Lord, let us shout aloud to the Rock of our Salvation" (Psalm 95:1).

In every generation new hymns have been written and published. Yet the oldest hymnbook of the church, the Psalter or Book of Psalms, has never lost its appeal.

Jesus Himself loved the Psalms. He often quoted them. He also applied some of them to Himself. He was David's son and lord (Psalm 110), He said, and the rejected stone which became the building's capstone (Psalm 118). He also saw Himself as experiencing the terrible sufferings of the innocent victim who is depicted, for example, in Psalms 22, 31, 41 and 59.

The reason why Christian people are drawn to the psalms is that they speak the universal language of the human soul. "The Book of Psalms," wrote Rowland E.Prothero in *The Psalms in Human Life* (1904) "contains the whole music of the heart of man." Whatever our spiritual mood may be, there is sure to be a psalm which reflects it – whether triumph or defeat, excitement or depression, joy or sorrow, praise or penitence, wonder or anger. Above all, the psalms declare the greatness of the living God as Creator, Sustainer, King, Lawgiver, Saviour, Father, Shepherd and Judge. As we come to know Him better through the Psalter, we fall down and worship Him.

A book called *The Canticles and Selected Psalms* was published in 1966 in Hodder and Stoughton's series of "Prayer Book Commentaries". It has long been out of print. I am therefore grateful to Tim Dowley for proposing the modernization and re-publication of some of the expositions in this beautifully illustrated edition.

John Stott
February 1988

Psalm 1

The Way of the Righteous and the Wicked

Jerome quoted the opinion of some that this first psalm is "the preface of the Holy Spirit" to the Psalter. It is certainly a very apt introduction. Two particular themes are found in it, which recur in many other psalms.

The first is the clear-cut distinction between *the righteous* and *the wicked*. The Bible as a whole, and specially the Wisdom Literature, divides humankind into these two absolute categories, and does not recognise a third. Psalms 32, 36 and 112 also compare and contrast the righteous and the wicked.

The second theme concerns the present fortunes and the ultimate destinies of human beings. The first and last words of Psalm 1 indicate the alternatives. *Blessed* is the righteous person who delights in God's law; the ungodly, on the other hand, will *perish*. This process of "blessing" and "cursing," as Jeremiah called it when he perhaps elaborated this psalm (see Jeremiah 17:5-8), is already discernible in this life.

The West Wall, or Wailing Wall, Jerusalem, which gets its name from the lamentation of the Jews for the destruction of the Temple. It was the only part of the Temple that was almost always accessible to them.

In handling these two themes the author of Psalm 1 is only anticipating what Jesus Himself was to teach, that men and women are either on the broad road that leads to destruction or on the narrow way that leads to life (Matthew 7:13, 14).

The righteous will prosper (verses 1-4)

The righteous person is described first negatively, then positively. He or she *does not walk in the counsel of the wicked or stand in the way of sinners or sit in the seat of mockers.* These expressions have been carefully composed in a triple set of parallels: "walk, stand, sit," "counsel, way, seat," and "wicked, sinners, mockers." Moreover, a downward progression is implied. The godly do not model their conduct on the

¹Blessed is the man
　who does not walk in the counsel of
　　the wicked
　or stand in the way of sinners
　or sit in the seat of mockers.

²But his delight is in the law of the LORD,
　and on his law he meditates day and
　　night.

³He is like a tree planted by streams of
　　water,
　which yields its fruit in season
　and whose leaf does not wither.
　Whatever he does prospers.

⁴Not so the wicked!
　They are like the chaff
　that the wind blows away.

⁵Therefore the wicked will not stand in
　　the judgment,
　nor sinners in the assembly of the
　　righteous.

⁶For the LORD watches over the way of
　　the righteous,
　but the way of the wicked will perish.

advice of bad people. Further, the godly do not linger in the company of persistent evildoers; still less remain permanently among the cynical who openly scoff at God.

Instead of taking the lead from such people, the godly make *the law of the LORD* their rule (verse 2). This *law (Torah)* refers not just to the Ten Commandments, or even all the rules and regulations of the law of Moses, but to all God's revelation as the guide of life, which, although given through Moses and the prophets, is yet *the law of the LORD,* a phrase virtually equivalent to "the word of God".

The law of the Lord is the righteous person's *delight.* This is an indication of new birth, for "...the sinful mind is hostile to God. It does not submit to God's law, nor can it do so" (Romans 8:7). As a result of the inward, regenerating work of the Holy Spirit, however, the godly find that they love the law of God simply because it conveys to them the will of their God. They do not rebel against its exacting demands; their whole being approves and endorses it (see Psalms 19; 40:8; 112:1; 119). Delighting in it, the godly will *meditate* in it, or pore over it, constantly, day and night.

It is believed that this was the favorite text of Jerome, the author of the old Latin version of the Bible. He certainly exemplified it in his life, relentlessly pursuing his study of the Scriptures first in the desert, and then for nearly thirty-five years in his grotto near the traditional scene of the Nativity in Bethlehem. Indeed, all Christians know something of the psalmist's experience. To them daily meditation in the Bible is an unending delight.

This, then, is the characteristic of the righteous. For guidance regarding daily conduct they look not to public opinion, the unreliable fashions of the godless world, but to the revealed Word of God, in which they delight and meditate. As a result they are *like a tree planted by streams of water* (verse 3).

The metaphor is a common one in the Bible. Whatever kind of tree is in mind, it clearly enjoys the secret of perennial health and vigour, its fruit ripening in its season, and its leaf not withering even under the heat of the sun; for as the tree draws constant nourishment from the water through its roots, so through daily meditation in the law of the Lord the righteous refresh and replenish their soul in God. Such a tree is firmly *planted*; such people, like Joshua, prosper in whatever they do.

The ungodly will perish (verses 5, 6)
Not so the wicked! Their present condition and future destiny are entirely different. Instead of being like a fruitful tree, they are like dry and useless chaff. Instead of being planted by the waterside, they are driven by the wind.

Again, the metaphor was a familiar one in Bible days and

A pious Jew reads from the Scriptures at the Wailing Wall, Jerusalem. Since 1967 the area in front of the wall has been opened out into a large public square.

Bible lands (compare Psalm 35:5; Isaiah 17:13; Matthew 3:12). The threshing floor was usually a hard, flat surface situated on a hill, well exposed to the wind. The wheat was lifted by large winnowing fans or shovels and thrown into the air, so that the precious grain would drop down and be garnered, while the light husks of the chaff would be scattered to the four winds.

The wicked *are like chaff* in two senses. They are desiccated and unprofitable in themselves; and they are easily blown away by the judgment of God. The basic idea behind the Hebrew word for *the wicked* appears to be one of "restlessness" (compare Isaiah 57:20,21). The tree is planted firmly; but the chaff is unstable. When God begins to sift them in His present activity of judgment, and specially when the final day of judgment comes, they will not stand. Not even now can they stand *in the assembly of the righteous,* for they do not belong to the godly remnant of His people.

Verse 6 is a general conclusion to the whole psalm, distinguishing between *the way of the righteous* and *the way of the wicked.* We are told that the Lord *watches over the way of the righteous;* whereas *the way of the wicked will perish.*

Psalm 8

What is a Human Being?

"This short, exquisite lyric," as it was called by C.S.Lewis, begins and ends with the refrain: *O LORD, our Lord, how majestic is your name in all the earth.* Here is a recognition of the majesty of God's name, or nature, which His works reveal in both earth and heaven. The enemies of God, blinded by their proud rebellion, do not see His glory; but they are confounded by *children and infants.* Jesus quoted these words when the children acclaimed Him in the Temple with their hosannas, while the chief priests and scribes indignantly objected (Matthew 21:15,16). God is still glorified in the simple faith of children and in the childlike humility of Christian believers (see Matthew 11:25,26; 1 Corinthians 1:26-29).

---

[1]O LORD, our Lord,
how majestic is your name in all the earth!

You have set your glory above the heavens.
[2]From the lips of children and infants you have ordained praise because of your enemies, to silence the foe and the avenger.

[3]When I consider your heavens, the work of your fingers, the moon and the stars, which you have set in place,
[4]what is man that you are mindful of him, the son of man that you care for him?

What particularly evokes the wondering worship of the psalmist is God's condescension toward human beings (verses 3,4) and the position of dominion which He has granted to them on earth (verses 5-8). Seen in relation to each other, these two truths enable us to have a balanced judgment of humankind and to give a proper answer to the psalmist's rhetorical question, *What is man?* (verse 4), that is, What does it mean to be a human being?.

The littleness of human beings (verses 3,4)

The question was prompted by a consideration of the night sky. If David was the author of this psalm, there can be little doubt that he was referring to the experience of his youth. In his shepherd days, tending his father's flock in the hills near Bethlehem, he often slept under the stars. Lying on his back, he would survey the fathomless immensity above him, seeking to penetrate the clear depths of the eastern sky. He recognised that the heavens, with the moon and the stars, were the work

---

[5]You made him a little lower than the heavenly beings
and crowned him with glory and honour.

[6]You made him ruler over the works of your hands;
you put everything under his feet:
[7]all flocks and herds,
and beasts of the field,

[8]the birds of the air,
and fish of the sea,
all that swim the paths of the seas.

[9]O LORD, our Lord,
how majestic is your name in all the earth!

of God's fingers (verse 3), and as he contemplated their greatness and mystery, he cried out: *What is man that you are mindful of him, and the son of man that you care for him?* (verse 4).

If this was David's reaction, nearly three thousand years ago, how much more should it be ours who live in days of astro-physics and the conquest of space? As we consider the orbiting planets of our solar system, so infinitesimally small in comparison with countless galaxies millions of light years distant, it may seem to us incredible that the great God of the universe should take any note of us at all, let alone *care for* us. Yet He does; and Jesus assured us that even the hairs of our head are all numbered.

The greatness of human beings (verses 5-8)
The psalmist moves from the littleness of a human being, in comparison with the vastness of the universe, to the greatness which God has given him on earth: *You made him a little lower than the heavenly beings and crowned him with glory and honor. You made him ruler over the works of your hands* (verses 5,6).

Our position of only slight inferiority to the heavenly beings, or even to God Himself, is supremely seen in our *rule*. God has invested human beings with royal sovereignty, crowning us with glory and honor (verse 5) and delegating to us the control of His works. It is even stated that God has put *everything... under his* (man's) *feet.*

The psalmist is referring primarily to the animal creation – beasts both domesticated and wild, *the birds of the air, and the fish of the sea,* and all other creatures inhabiting the depths of the ocean (verses 7,8). This is not poetic fiction. As the universe yields more and more of its secrets to scientific research, so our dominion increases. Yet even now humankind is not, in fact, lord of creation, with *everything* under our feet, as is recognised in the three New Testament quotations of these verses.

According to Hebrews 2:5 and the following verses: "... at present we do not see everything subject to him." It is immediately added, however: "But we see Jesus, who was made a little lower than the angels, now crowned with glory and honour." Humankind has sinned and fallen, and consequently has lost some of the dominion which God had given us; but in Jesus, the second Adam, this dominion has been restored. It is in Him rather than in us that humankind's dominion is exhibited. By His death He even destroyed the devil and delivered his slaves (verses 14, 15). He has now been "crowned", and exalted to God's right hand.

Although the Psalm's description of humankind's dominion is true rather of the man Christ Jesus than of us, it applies to us also if we have come by faith to share in His exaltation. The apostle Paul wrote that the exceeding greatness of God's power, which exalted Jesus and "put everything under his feet," is available to us who believe (Ephesians 1:19-22). Indeed, we have experienced it, for it has raised us from the death of sin, exalted us with Christ and made us sit with Him in the heavenly places, where we are partakers of his victory and dominion (Ephesians 2:5,6).

Even this is not the end. Although Christ is exalted far above all rule and authority, and all things are potentially under His feet, not all His enemies have yet conceded their defeat or surrendered to Him. Only when He appears in glory and the dead rise, will He destroy "all dominion, authority and power. For he must reign until he has put all his enemies under his feet. The last enemy to be destroyed is death. For He 'has put every thing under his feet'" (1 Corinthians 15:24-26).

A young Jewish boy reads the Scriptures at the synagogue at the Wailing Wall, Jerusalem. The synagogue is near the so-called Wilson Arch, once an entrance to the Temple.

13

Opposite: Orthodox Jews
pray at the Western Wall,
Jerusalem. Many of them
wear the characteristic
black coats and hats of
their ancestors in Eastern
Europe.

Psalm 15

An Uncorrupt Life

Psalm 15 is concerned with the conditions on which a man or woman may dwell with God. It is especially noteworthy because it unites religion and morality in an indissoluble partnership. It opens with a question, continues with an answer to the question posed, and concludes with a grand assertion which goes beyond the terms of the original question.

The question (verse 1)

Lord, who may dwell in your sanctuary? Who may live on your holy hill? God's *holy hill* was of course Jerusalem and his *sanctuary* probably the tent which housed the ark before Solomon built the Temple. Indeed, it has generally been thought that this psalm, like Psalm 24, refers to the occasion, described in 2 Samuel 6:12-19 and 1 Chronicles 15 and 16, when David brought the ark from the house of Obed-edom on to Mount Zion, "the city of David," and placed it in the tent which he had pitched for it. In this case, the psalm outlines the moral challenge which God's presence in their midst brought to the inhabitants of Jerusalem.

But the psalm has a wider application than this. It inquires into the terms on which any human being may dwell in God's

¹LORD, who may dwell in your
      sanctuary?
  Who may live on your holy hill?

²He whose walk is blameless
    and who does what is righteous,
who speaks the truth from his heart
³   and has no slander on his tongue,
who does his neighbour no wrong
    and casts no slur on his fellow man,
⁴who despises a vile man
    but honours those who fear the
      LORD,
who keeps his oath
    even when it hurts,
⁵who lends his money without usury
    and does not accept a bribe against
      the innocent.

He who does these things
  will never be shaken.

An Arab merchant in the
vegetable market in
Bethlehem.

presence, either in this life or in the life to come. The psalmist
is clear that Jehovah is a holy God and that sinners separate
themselves from God by their sin. "You are not a God who
takes pleasure in evil; with you the wicked cannot dwell"
(Psalm 5:4). Who, then, may dwell with God?

The answer (verses 2-6)

The psalmist now answers his own question and describes the
kind of person who may draw near to God. He paints an
attractive picture. Indeed, no one has perfectly fulfilled this
ideal except the man Christ Jesus. Jesus Christ alone has

entered the presence of God in heaven in virtue of His own merit; for us access to God is possible only through Christ.

But, having been brought near to God by Christ, we can enjoy continuing fellowship with Him only if by His grace we lead the kind of holy life which this psalm depicts. It is a social holiness. That is, it concerns entirely our duty to our neighbor, since we cannot have a right relationship with God without a right relationship with human beings. We cannot expect to dwell in God's presence if we are not seeking our neighbor's good.

So the people who may enjoy God's company are described as *blameless* (verse 2). They are people of such complete integrity of character that they both do what is right and speak what is true. Further, the truth they speak is from their *heart,* for they always mean what they say. They are thus consistent in thought, word, and deed.

This general and positive statement is now illustrated by particular and largely negative examples. Indeed, it is against the background of these negatives that the positive excellence of good people stands out in shining relief.

First, they do not harm their neighbors by anything they say or do (verse 3). They neither slander them, nor wrong them, nor cast slurs against them. This last expression probably means either that they do not repeat gossip about their neighbors, or that they do not take unfair advantage of them when they are overtaken by adversity. Secondly, they are discerning in their assessment of others (verse 4). They are not afraid to express disapproval of worthless people. Thirdly, they are faithful to their promises, even when it is to their own inconvenience or disadvantage. They are people of their word (verse 5). Fourthly, they never exploit the poor or oppress the innocent (verse 6).

More precisely, they do not lend money on usury or accept bribes. We are introduced here to familiar figures in the Old Testament – the extortionate moneylender and the unjust magistrate who perverts justice for a bribe. Both practices were forbidden by the law (Exodus 22:25; Leviticus 25:35-38 and Exodus 23:6-8; Deuteronomy 16:19; 27:25) and denounced by the prophets (see, for example, Ezekiel 22:12).

The assertion (verse 7)

The psalmist has asked who shall dwell in God's presence, and has answered his own question by portraying a person who loves his or her neighbor. But he does not stop there. Such people, he concludes, will not only abide in God's sanctuary; they *will never be shaken.* On the contrary, they will remain firm and secure throughout all the vicissitudes of this life, and on the day of judgment.

17

Psalm 16

Present Faith and Future Hope

Although this psalm opens with a prayer (*Keep me safe, O God*), it is in reality a believer's testimony regarding both his present faith and his future hope. Having taken refuge in God (verse 1), he has found in Him his greatest good (verses 2,6,7) and is convinced that even death cannot rob him of that true life which consists of fellowship with God (verses 11,12). These final verses were applied to the resurrection of Jesus Christ by Peter on the day of Pentecost and by Paul in the synagogue of Antioch in Pisidia (Acts 2:24-31; 13:34-37).

Present faith (verses 1-6)
What it means to put one's trust in God, or to *take refuge* (verse 1) in Him, is explained in verse 2 (compare Psalm 73:24). The believer has turned from the pleasures of sin and the vanities of the world to seek and find his good in God. Delighting in God, he delights also in the godly, the *saints* (verse 3).

In the ungodly, however, who have exchanged the true and living God for *other gods* (verse 4), the believer takes no delight. He knows that they will have great trouble – their *sorrows... will increase*. He affirms with resolve that he will neither offer their idolatrous libations of blood nor even mention the names of their false deities (verse 5). To do so would be incompatible with his wholehearted devotion to the Lord, of whom he now writes in the most exalted terms (verses 5,6).

¹Keep me safe, O God,
    for in you I take refuge.

²I said to the LORD, "You are my Lord;
    apart from you I have no good thing."
³As for the saints who are in the land,
    they are the glorious ones in whom
    is all my delight.
⁴The sorrows of those will increase
    who run after other gods.
I will not pour out their libations of blood
    or take up their names on my lips.

⁵LORD, you have assigned me my
    portion and my cup;
    you have made my lot secure.
⁶The boundary lines have fallen for me
    in pleasant places;
    surely I have a delightful inheritance.

⁷I praise the LORD, who counsels me;
    even at night my heart instructs me.
⁸I have set the LORD always before me.
    Because he is at my right hand,
    I shall not be shaken.

⁹Therefore my heart is glad and my
    tongue rejoices;
    my body also will rest secure,
¹⁰because you will not abandon me to
    the grave,
    nor will you let your Holy One see
    decay.
¹¹You have made known to me the path
    of life;
    you will fill me with joy in your
    presence,
    with eternal pleasures at your right
    hand.

The Garden Tomb, East Jerusalem. Though it is most unlikely that Jesus was buried and arose from this tomb, many visitors find this garden a haven of tranquility.

The Lord has assigned him his *portion* (alluding probably to a portion of food rather than of land) and his *cup*, thus both satisfying his hunger and quenching his thirst. Further, he has found God to be a *delightful inheritance*, just like the Levitical priests, who were given no inheritance in Canaan because their inheritance was the Lord (see, for example, Numbers 18:20).

Future hope (verses 7-11)

David, who according to the apostles Peter and Paul was the author of this psalm, now breaks out into thanksgiving (verse 7) that the Lord has given him *counsel* and that *at night* his *heart instructs* him. What this divine instruction is which he has received he does not make clear. It seems best to refer it to the remaining verses of the psalm.

God draws near to David and speaks to him; his own heart teaches him while in the stillness of the night he meditates on his intimate fellowship with God. He learns to draw from his experience this mighty deduction: that because God is ever before him and beside him (verse 8), *I shall not be shaken.* In other words, the blessings of his communion with God cannot be limited to his satisfaction only; they include his security also. His present faith brings a future hope.

David now rejoices in heart and soul because he is convinced that his body also may *rest secure* (verse 9). He goes on to elaborate his new assurance in direct speech to God (verses 11,12).

Three levels of interpretation are possible in these verses, all of which are true. Literally they express the writer's confidence that he will not die, that his soul will not be delivered *to the grave* – the translation of the Hebrew *sheol,* the abode of the dead. Nor will his body *see decay.* We do not know the historical circumstances in which the psalm was written, but it may possibly express the confidence which sustained David during his months as an outlaw, that he would not be delivered into the hand of Saul.

The implication of these verses goes further than this, however. The corollary to deliverance from death is treading *the path of life*; and this life is seen to be no mere physical survival, but the enjoyment of God's presence bringing *joy* and *eternal pleasures.* It is in fact what the New Testament calls "eternal life," communion with God, which physical death cannot interrupt. It is unlikely that David understood fully what he was writing, since life and immortality were only clearly revealed by Jesus Christ (2 Timothy 1:10); yet his words find their true fulfillment only in the consummation of eternal life beyond the grave.

When Peter applied these verses to the resurrection of Jesus, he went so far as to say that David cannot have been referring primarily to himself, since he died and was buried. He went on: "But he was a prophet and knew that God had promised him on oath that he would place one of his descendants on his throne. Seeing what was ahead, he spoke of the resurrection of the Christ, that he was not abandoned to the grave, nor did his body see decay" (Acts 2:30,31).

We must be careful not to make Peter say more than he actually did say. He himself in his first letter (1 Peter 1:10-12) explained that the prophets did not fully understand to what the Spirit of Christ within them was referring when predicting Christ's sufferings and subsequent glory. We need not therefore assert that David was making a deliberate and conscious prophecy of the resurrection of Jesus which was fully intelligible to himself. It is enough to say that, caught up by the Spirit of prophecy, he was led to write words about the conquest of death and the fulness of life and joy in the presence of God, which would be finally fulfilled not in his own experience but in that of his illustrious descendant.

Psalm 19
The Self-Revelation of God

According to C.S.Lewis, this is "the greatest poem in the Psalter and one of the greatest lyrics in the world." From the Christian point of view it contains the clearest summary of the doctrine of revelation to be found in the Old Testament, namely that God has made Himself known to all humankind as Creator (verses 1-6), to Israel as Lawgiver (verses 7-10), and to the individual as Redeemer (verses 11-14).

General revelation (verses 1-6)
Human beings cannot plead ignorance of God, since He never ceases to give a revelation of Himself, which is called "general" because it is made to all people everywhere. As the apostle Paul put it, he has not "left himself without testimony" (Acts 14:17; compare Acts 17:22-28 and Romans 1:20).

This witness is in nature, especially here *the heavens*, which *declare the glory of God* because they are *the work of his hands* (verse 1). Even more today, through the cosmology of modern astrophysics, the heavens, "their vastness, splendor, order and mystery" as one commentator puts it, reveal God's glory and greatness.

God's witness to Himself through the heavens has three characteristics. First, it is continuous. *Day after day... night after night* (verse 2) the testimony is given without intermission. Secondly, it is abundant. The verb in verse 2 is expressive: *they* (the heavens) *pour forth speech*. Thirdly it is universal. Although *there is no speech or language* (verse 3), yet by sight rather than sound their message penetrates to the end of the world (verse 4). Paul even applies this last verse to the worldwide spread of the gospel (Romans 10:18).

Of this universal witness to God by the heavens, the sun is a particular example. In dramatic imagery, which is not of course intended to be taken literally, the psalmist likens the sunrise to the emergence of a bridegroom from his chamber, and its daily course across the sky to the running of an athlete, so that *nothing is hidden from its heat* (verse 6).

Special revelation (verses 7-10)
Abruptly and without warning the subject changes from God's general and natural revelation through creation to His special and supernatural revelation through *torah*, "the law," which

Sunset over the Sea of
Galilee. "The heavens
declare the glory of God;
the skies proclaim the
work of his hands."

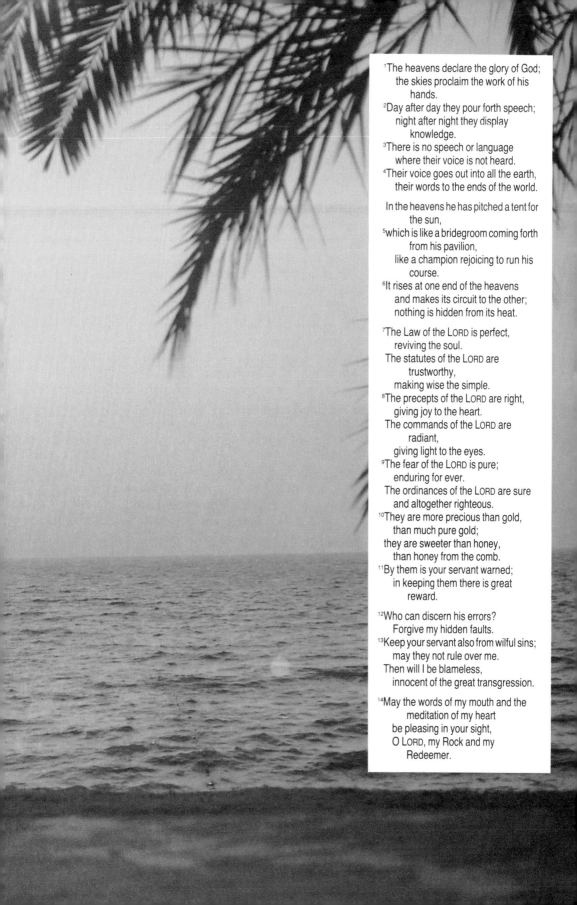

¹The heavens declare the glory of God;
   the skies proclaim the work of his
      hands.
²Day after day they pour forth speech;
   night after night they display
      knowledge.
³There is no speech or language
   where their voice is not heard.
⁴Their voice goes out into all the earth,
   their words to the ends of the world.

In the heavens he has pitched a tent for
      the sun,
⁵which is like a bridegroom coming forth
      from his pavilion,
   like a champion rejoicing to run his
      course.
⁶It rises at one end of the heavens
   and makes its circuit to the other;
   nothing is hidden from its heat.

⁷The Law of the LORD is perfect,
   reviving the soul.
The statutes of the LORD are
      trustworthy,
   making wise the simple.
⁸The precepts of the LORD are right,
   giving joy to the heart.
The commands of the LORD are
      radiant,
   giving light to the eyes.
⁹The fear of the LORD is pure;
   enduring for ever.
The ordinances of the LORD are sure
   and altogether righteous.
¹⁰They are more precious than gold,
   than much pure gold;
they are sweeter than honey,
   than honey from the comb.
¹¹By them is your servant warned;
   in keeping them there is great
      reward.

¹²Who can discern his errors?
   Forgive my hidden faults.
¹³Keep your servant also from wilful sins;
   may they not rule over me.
Then will I be blameless,
   innocent of the great transgression.

¹⁴May the words of my mouth and the
      meditation of my heart
   be pleasing in your sight,
   O LORD, my Rock and my
      Redeemer.

refers not merely to the law of Moses but to all Old Testament Scripture. The transition, though abrupt, is not arbitrary. The heavens and the law both make God known. Further, C.S.Lewis may be right to detect a link in the reference to the all-pervasive heat of the sun, so that "the searching and cleansing sun becomes an image of the searching and cleansing law."

With the change of subject comes a significant change in the divine name. The One who reveals Himself in nature to all people is *God*, Hebrew *El* (verse 1), the God of creation; but it is the LORD Yahweh (seven times in the second half of the psalm), the God of the covenant, who has revealed Himself through His law to His covenant people Israel. It is a revelation not now of His glory but of His will, and its excellencies are set forth in perfect Hebrew parallelism (verses 7-9).

The symmetry of these verses is so precise that each begins with a different aspect of God's will, and goes on to describe both what it is and what it does. Thus, *the law*, or divine instruction, is *perfect*, bearing witness to God's nature expressed in His will, and consists of particular *statutes, precepts*, and *commands*. Its perfection is seen in the fact that its injunctions are *trustworthy, right, radiant, pure, sure and altogether righteous*. It is also called *the fear of the* LORD (verse 9) because the great end of all revelation is to inspire a humble and reverent worship of God. This disclosure of God's will is said to be *pure*.

But the psalmist does not merely contemplate the law of the Lord as it is in itself; he also unfolds its beneficial effects, *reviving the soul,* rejoicing the heart and, above all, *making wise* (verse 7) and *giving light* (verse 8) to those who are humble enough, or (as our Lord was later to teach) childlike enough, to receive it. The inherent qualities and health-giving results of God's law make it *more precious than gold... sweeter... than honey from the comb* (verse 10).

It may be surprising to us that the writer did not find God's law a burden to him; we may feel with C.S.Lewis that his reference to its sweetness is at first sight "very mysterious," even "utterly bewildering." The explanation is not just that its commandments were right, nor that its promises were sure, but that it was the revelation of God, the special means which He had chosen to make Himself known to His people Israel.

Personal revelation (verses 11-14)
With verse 11 the psalmist for the first time mentions himself. He has been describing how *all the earth* (verse 4) may apprehend God's glory from nature, and how *the simple* (verse 7) may derive wisdom from God's law. But he concludes his psalm by disclosing his personal spiritual aspirations as God's *servant* (verses 11,13).

A pilgrim to the Holy Land. "May the words of my mouth and the meditation of my heart be pleasing in your sight, O Lord, my Rock and my Redeemer."

He has himself found wholesome warning in God's law and knows that conformity to it brings great reward (verse 11). He seems to have discovered in his own experience the dual purpose of the divine law, namely to reveal sin (Romans 3:20) and to promote holiness. This leads him both to pray for cleansing from the *hidden faults* (verse 12) which he has committed, and for deliverance from *wilful sins* (verse 13) which he longs to avoid, so that he is not mastered by them but is kept *innocent of great transgression*. The psalmist is not referring here to any one particularly grievous sin, or even the blasphemy against the Holy Spirit (as poor John Bunyan thought), but to all deliberate wrongdoing, sins committed "defiantly" (Numbers 15:30,31).

The psalm ends with a prayer which is frequently echoed by Christian ministers before they preach. In it the writer goes beyond his plea for deliverance, to a positive and very personal desire that all his words, and even his thoughts, shall be *pleasing* in the sight of God, whom he now declares to be both his *Rock* ("strength") and his *Redeemer*. Redemption is in itself negative deliverance from sin; it needs to be completed by a life that is pleasing to God (see Titus 2:14).

Opposite: Good Friday pilgrims carry a cross along the *Via Dolorosa* in Jerusalem, following the traditional route of Jesus on his way to the crucifixion.

Psalm 22

The Sufferings and Glory of Christ

This is the first of a number of so-called "passion psalms" in the Psalter, which describe the suffering and persecution of an innocent victim in terms reminiscent of the Suffering Servant of the Lord in the second part of Isaiah. Although some commentators have suggested that the godly sufferer is more ideal than real, representing perhaps the Israelite nation when exiled among the heathen, the narrative of his afflictions is so vivid in its details that it undoubtedly depicts a true and literal experience.

¹My God, my God, why have you
    forsaken me?
  Why are you so far from saving me,
    so far from the words of my
    groaning?
²O my God, I cry out by day, but you do
    not answer,
  by night, and am not silent.

³Yet you are enthroned as the Holy One;
  you are the praise of Israel.
⁴In you our fathers put their trust;
  they trusted you and you delivered
    them.
⁵They cried to you and were saved;
  in you they trusted and were not
    disappointed.

⁶But I am a worm and not a man,
  scorned by men and despised by
    people.
⁷All who see me mock me;
  they hurl insults, shaking their
    heads:
⁸"He trusts in the LORD;
  let the LORD rescue him.
  Let him deliver him,
    since he delights in him."

⁹Yet you brought me out of the womb;
  you made me trust in you
    even at my mother's breast.
¹⁰From birth I was cast upon you;
  from my mother's womb you have
    been my God.
¹¹Do not be far from me,
  for trouble is near
  and there is no-one to help.

¹²Many bulls surround me;
  strong bulls of Bashan encircle me.
¹³Roaring lions tearing their prey
  open their mouths wide against me.
¹⁴I am poured out like water,
  and all my bones are out of joint.
  My heart has turned to wax;
    it has melted away within me.
¹⁵My strength is dried up like a potsherd,
  and my tongue sticks to the roof of
    my mouth;
  you lay me in the dust of death.
¹⁶Dogs have surrounded me;
  a band of evil men has encircled me,
  they have pierced my hands and
    feet.
¹⁷I can count all my bones;
  people stare and gloat over me.
¹⁸They divide my garments among them
  and cast lots for my clothing.

¹⁹But you, O LORD, be not far off;
  O my Strength, come quickly to help
    me.
²⁰Deliver my life from the sword,
  my precious life from the power of
    the dogs.
²¹Rescue me from the mouth of the lions;
  save me from the horns of wild oxen.

²²I will declare your name to my brothers;
  in the congregation I will praise you.
²³You who fear the LORD, praise him!
  All you descendants of Jacob,
    honour him!
  Revere him, all you descendants of
    Israel!

²⁴For he has not despised or disdained
  the suffering of the afflicted one;
  he has not hidden his face from him
  but has listened to his cry for help.

²⁵From you comes my praise in the great
    assembly;
  before those who fear you, will I fulfil
    my vows.
²⁶The poor will eat and be satisfied;
  they who seek the LORD will praise
    him –
  may your hearts live for ever!
²⁷All the ends of the earth
  will remember and turn to the LORD,
  and all the families of the nations
  will bow down before him,
²⁸for dominion belongs to the LORD,
  and he rules over nations.

²⁹All the rich of the earth will feast and
    worship;
  all who go down to the dust will kneel
    before him –
  those who cannot keep themselves
    alive.
³⁰Posterity will serve him;
  future generations will be told about
    the LORD.
³¹They will proclaim his righteousness
  to a people yet unborn –
  for he has done it.

Yet Christian eyes cannot read this psalm, nor Christian lips sing it, without applying it to the sufferings of Christ and His subsequent glory. Not only did Jesus quote its opening words as one of His seven sayings from the cross (Matthew 27:46; Mark 15:34), but the mockery of verses 7 and 8 was echoed by the priests (Matthew 27:39-44; Mark 15:31-32; Luke 23:35), the division of clothing in verse 18 was said to be fulfilled by the soldiers (John 19:23,24), and verse 22 is applied to Christ in Hebrews 2:11,12. Further, the sufferer's agony in verses 14 to 17 — his disjointed bones, his thirst and his pierced hands and feet — is a remarkable description of the horrors of crucifixion, although it is not quoted of Christ in the New Testament.

The psalm is in two contrasting parts.

The cry of anguish (verses 1-21)
The sufferer cries out to God in an agonised question: *Why have you forsaken me?* His greatest suffering is neither the physical pain, nor the mockery of his persecutors, which he will later describe, but his sense of God-forsakenness. His question is asked in perplexity, not in despair or bitterness. Indeed, the poignancy of his condition is that he continues in faith to appeal to God three times as *my God* even while he is forsaken and receives no reply.

Three thoughts seem to aggravate his condition and at the same time buttress his faith. He expresses them in the next paragraphs. First, there was the experience of the ancients (verses 3-5). He knows that God is *holy*, separate from and exalted above all other beings, because the fathers trusted in Him and cried to Him, and they were delivered, *not disappointed.* Secondly, there are the taunts of his enemies (verses 6-8), who mock him because his experience is not like that of the fathers: *He trusts in the Lord; let the Lord rescue him.* Will God allow them thus to blaspheme Him? Thirdly, the psalmist looks back to his own past experience of God (verses 9-11). Jehovah has been his God from his birth; He will surely not abandon him now. These thoughts lead him to a piteous appeal to God (verse 11) that he will not be far away, since trouble is close at hand.

What precisely is his *trouble*? He is evidently very sick, indeed dying, fast approaching *the dust of death* (verse 15). He portrays the physical symptoms he both sees and feels (verses 14,15).

But his bodily pains are made worse by the *band of evil men* (verse 16) who surround him. He has already likened them to *strong bulls* from the rich pasture-land of Bashan and to lions ready to devour him (verses 12,13). Now he pictures them as savage pariah *dogs* (verse 16), and later as *wild oxen* (verse 21) waiting to tear him limb from limb. In some brutal way they pierce his hands and feet; they *stare and gloat* over him (verse 17); they even strip him of his clothes and share them out (verse 18), or have done so mentally in anticipation of his death. For the third time (see verses 1,2, and 11) he appeals to God to draw near to him in his need and to deliver him (verses 19-21).

The song of praise (verses 22-31)
Suddenly and dramatically the tone of the psalm changes from prayer to praise, from suffering to triumph. God's deliverance of the sufferer is not described. We are simply told (verse 24) that in the end God has *not despised* His afflicted servant, as men had despised him (verse 6), but has heard his cry when he called to Him. The psalmist's soul is so transported with adoration that he wants everybody to praise God with him. The true worshipper is always thus missionary-minded; he cannot conceive of praising God alone. In the remaining verses of the psalm the circle of those who are summoned to the worship of God grows ever wider until finally it embraces all nations and all ages.

First, he will declare and praise God's name in the great assembly (verses 22-25). He means to bear public witness to God's deliverance among his fellow Israelites, the *descendants of Jacob*, and offer Him public praise. Next, he seems to think of his fellow-sufferers, others who are still *poor* (verse 26) or "afflicted" (Revised Standard Version) as he has been (verse 24). He wants them to share his joy and with him *eat and be satisfied*, probably in the sacrifical meal which followed a thank-offering. Next (verses 27,28) his prophetic eyes look on to the conversion of the nations, and he asserts that *All the ends of the earth will... turn to the* LORD, recognising that universal *dominion belongs* to him.

Even this glorious prospect does not exhaust his vision. Although verse 29 is acknowledged as obscure and may bring together either the proud and the humble who realise their mortality, or the living and the dead, yet verses 30 and 31 contain a clear reference to the psalmist's *posterity*. They too, a *people yet unborn*, shall hear of the Lord and of His salvation. Thus, the publishing of the gospel of salvation is to be both universal and everlasting, and we see dimly foreshadowed in the results of this godly man's sufferings the final triumph of the Crucified.

Psalm 23

The Lord is My Shepherd

There are, in this best known and best loved of all psalms, two graphic pictures of God's intimate relationship with one of His people. The first is the shepherd and his sheep, the second the host and his guest.

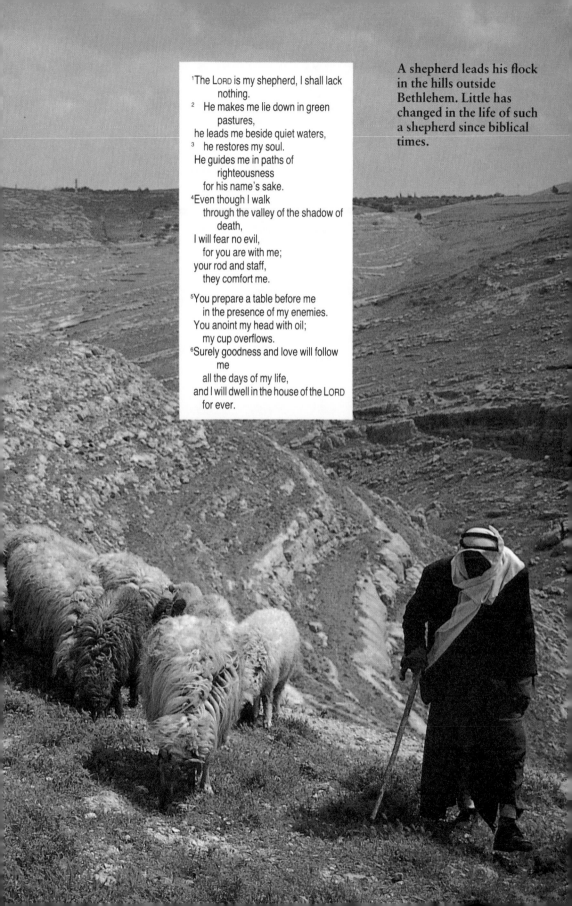

¹The Lᴏʀᴅ is my shepherd, I shall lack
 nothing.
²   He makes me lie down in green
      pastures,
he leads me beside quiet waters,
³   he restores my soul.
He guides me in paths of
   righteousness
   for his name's sake.
⁴Even though I walk
   through the valley of the shadow of
      death,
I will fear no evil,
   for you are with me;
your rod and staff,
   they comfort me.

⁵You prepare a table before me
   in the presence of my enemies.
You anoint my head with oil;
   my cup overflows.
⁶Surely goodness and love will follow
      me
   all the days of my life,
and I will dwell in the house of the Lᴏʀᴅ
   for ever.

A shepherd leads his flock
in the hills outside
Bethlehem. Little has
changed in the life of such
a shepherd since biblical
times.

The Lord my shepherd (verses 1-4)

It was natural for a pastoral community to think of the Lord as their shepherd, who *brought his people out like a flock; he led them like sheep through the desert* (Psalm 78:52; see also Psalm 80:1; Isaiah 40:11). But here the metaphor is made unmistakably personal. *The LORD is my shepherd*, the writer boldly claims, and does not even mention the other sheep of the flock.

The Christian cannot read or sing this psalm without thinking of Jesus Christ, who dared to reapply the metaphor from Jehovah to Himself. It is He who is to us "the good shepherd," "the Chief Shepherd," and "that great Shepherd of the sheep" (John 10:11,14; 1 Peter 5:4; Hebrews 13:20).

Once I can say from personal experience *the LORD is my shepherd*, I can add with assurance the consequence: *I shall lack nothing*. The Good Shepherd cares for His sheep and so provides for all my needs. He makes me lie down in green pastures to satisfy my hunger, and leads me beside refreshing waters to quench my thirst (verse 2). *For his name's sake*, that is, out of loyalty to His character and promises, He will guide me *in the paths of righteousness;* that is, He will not allow me to go astray (verse 3).

Indeed, even when I walk *through the darkest valley* (alternative translation, verse 4), whether that be death or some other sombre place, I have nothing to fear and I will not fear, because my Shepherd is *with me*, protecting me with His club and guiding me with His staff (verse 4). My security lies not, then, in my environment – whether green pastures and still waters or the darkest valley – but in my Shepherd. In His presence there is neither want (verse 1) nor fear (verse 4).

The Lord my host (verses 5,6)

The scene changes. I am no longer out of doors, but indoors; no longer a sheep in a flock, but a guest at a banquet. My divine host has prepared *a table before me*. It is not a secret feast, but enjoyed in the presence of my enemies, because when He satisfies the soul, it cannot be hidden from the world.

His provision is wonderfully lavish – a table laden with food, perfumed oils to anoint my head, and an overflowing cup (verse 5). Moreover, what God has begun He will surely continue. As He Himself will *lead me* (verses 2,3), so His *goodness and love will follow me*. Thus He will guard me behind and before, throughout *all the days of my life*. Finally, *I will dwell in the house of the LORD for ever* – not indeed in the Tabernacle or the Temple, nor even just in His presence in this life, but in that Father's house with its many mansions, of which Jesus spoke, where He said He was going to prepare a place for His own (John 14:1-4).

Psalm 24

Ascending the Hill of the Lord

The most probable historical setting for this psalm is the triumphant occasion described in 2 Samuel 6 when King David brought the ark from the house of Obed-edom into the tent which he had pitched for it in Jerusalem. It is probable that an annual Jewish festival commemorated either this event or God's choice of David and of Jerusalem, and that during it the ark was carried into the city and this psalm was sung.

Whatever the occasion, it is not difficult to imagine a processional choir singing it as they approached the Temple on Mount Zion, with the questions and answers of verses 3 and 4, and 7 to 10, chanted antiphonally as is sometimes done with effect by choirs today.

The whole earth (verses 1,2)
The psalm opens with a grand statement that the whole earth, with all its inhabitants, belongs to the Lord (verse 1) because He is its creator (verse 2): He has *founded it upon the seas* and *established it upon the waters*. This description of the land floating on the sea is of course poetic and is perhaps based on the account in Genesis 1 of the appearance of the dry land out of the sea. It is not misleading even today (figuratively speaking) when we consider that about seventy per cent of the earth's surface consists of water. The statement in verse 1 that the earth and its contents belong to God is quoted by Paul in 1 Corinthians 10:26 to support his argument that Christians may eat any food, even idol meats.

¹The earth is the LORD's, and
        everything in it,
    the world, and all who live in it;
²for he founded it upon the seas
    and established it upon the waters.

³Who may ascend the hill of the LORD?
    Who may stand in his holy place?
⁴He who has clean hands and a pure
        heart,
    who does not lift up his soul to an idol
    or swear by what is false.

⁵He will receive blessing from the LORD
        and vindication from God our
        Saviour.
⁶Such is the generation of those who
        seek him,
    who seek your face, O God of Jacob.
                                Selah

⁷Lift up your heads, O you gates;
    be lifted up, you ancient doors,
    that the King of glory may come in.
⁸Who is the King of glory?
    The LORD strong and mighty,
    the LORD mighty in battle.

⁹Lift up your heads, O you gates;
    lift them up, you ancient doors,
    that the King of glory may come in.
¹⁰Who is he, this King of glory?
    The LORD Almighty –
    he is the King of glory.   *Selah*

The Lord's hill (verses 3-6)

Although the whole earth is the Lord's, there is a certain hill which is His in a special sense. Called *the hill of the Lord* (verse 3) and *his holy place*, it is Mount Zion where the ark, the symbol of His presence, was housed. But *who may ascend* there into His holy presence (verse 3)? The answer, which is reminiscent of Psalm 15, expresses that union of worship and morality which is constantly insisted on in the Bible.

The only worship which is acceptable to God is that offered by people who have *clean hands and a pure heart* (verse 4), that is, who are holy in thought and motive as well as in deed.

The Dome of the Rock and the old city of Jerusalem from the Mount of Olives. The Dome of the Rock stands over the site of the Jewish Temple of biblical times.

Moreover, their holiness characterises their relationship with both God and others, for they do not *lift up (their) soul to an idol*, nor have they sworn *by what is false,* deceiving their neighbor. It is such people, godly and just, who will receive God's blessing and acceptance (verse 5); indeed, such blessing is the portion of all those *who seek your face, O God of Jacob* (verse 6).

The city gates (verses 7-10)

The procession bearing the ark has now reached the gates of the city of David, and the voices of the choir ring out: *Lift up your heads, O you gates... that the King of glory may come in* (verse 7). Back comes the challenge from inside the city: *Who is this King of glory?* to which the choir responds: *The LORD strong and mighty, the LORD mighty in battle* (verse 8). The whole dialogue is then repeated word for word (verses 9,10), except that in the final response *the King of glory* is now further described as *the LORD Almighty.* It is the first time that this title occurs in the Psalter, and it forms a splendid climax to this psalm.

Opposite: Waterfall at En Gedi, on the western shore of the Dead Sea. The Hebrew name means "Goats' Spring", and En Gedi was known well to the psalmist, David.

Psalm 27

The Soul's Changing Moods

The assertions and petitions of this psalm are made against the background of many enemies. If David was its author (which there seems no adequate reason to question), the situation described is likely to be either his pursuit by Saul or his flight from Absalom. In any case, the enemies are *evil men* (verse 2), persecuting him for righteousness' sake, and seeking to harm him by physical violence and by slander (verse 14). He likens them to wild beasts eager to tear him limb from limb (verse 2).

Confidence in God (verses 1-7)
The psalm opens with one of the most sublime Old Testament affirmations of the security of God's people. *The LORD is my light*, to guide me, *my salvation*, to deliver me, and *the stronghold of my life*, in whom I take refuge. *Of whom*, then, *shall*

¹The LORD is my light and my salvation –
   whom shall I fear?
The LORD is the stronghold of my life –
   of whom shall I be afraid?
²When evil men advance against me
   to devour my flesh,
when my enemies and my foes attack
      me,
   they will stumble and fall.
³Though an army besiege me,
   my heart will not fear;
though war break out against me,
   even then will I be confident.

⁴One thing I ask of the LORD,
   this is what I seek:
that I may dwell in the house of the
      LORD
   all the days of my life,
to gaze upon the beauty of the LORD
   and to seek him in his temple.
⁵For in the day of trouble
   he will keep me safe in his dwelling;
he will hide me in the shelter of his
      tabernacle
   and set me high upon a rock.
⁶Then my head will be exalted
   above the enemies who surround
      me;
at his tabernacle will I sacrifice with
      shouts of joy;
   I will sing and make music to the
      LORD.

⁷Hear my voice when I call, O LORD;
   be merciful to me and answer me.
⁸My heart says of you, "Seek his face!"
   Your face, LORD, I will seek.
⁹Do not hide your face from me,
   do not turn your servant away in
      anger;
   you have been my helper.
Do not reject me or forsake me,
   O God my Saviour.
¹⁰Though my father and mother forsake
      me,
   the LORD will receive me.
¹¹Teach me your way, O LORD;
   lead me in a straight path
   because of my oppressors.
¹²Do not hand me over to the desire of
      my foes,
   for false witnesses rise up against
      me,
   breathing out violence.

¹³I am still confident of this:
   I will see the goodness of the LORD
   in the land of the living.
¹⁴Wait for the LORD;
   be strong and take heart
   and wait for the LORD.

I be afraid? It is a defiant, unanswerable question reminiscent of those at the end of Romans 8. Let David's enemies attack him, yet *they will stumble and fall* (verse 2). Indeed (verse 3), if a whole army should make war against him, *even then* he will be *confident*.

Many Christians, surrounded by foes, have drawn strength from these words. One such was James Hannington, first Bishop of Equatorial Africa. In October 1885, on reaching Lake Victoria Nyanza, he was seized and imprisoned. "Consumed with fever, and at times delirious with pain, devoured by vermin, menaced every moment by the prospect of death, he found strength in the Psalms." On October 28, the day before he died a martyr's death, he wrote in his journal: "I am quite broken down and brought low. Comforted by Psalm 27."

This steadfast assurance of one man against many foes is now further explained. It lies in the presence and the protection of God. David cherishes one desire above all others (verse 4), namely to *dwell in the house of the LORD* all his life, so that he may both *gaze upon the beauty of the LORD* or "savour the sweetness of the Lord" and *seek him in his temple.*

It is most unlikely that we are intended to interpret this ambition literally. Only the priests lived in the precincts of God's house, whether what is here meant is the tabernacle at Shiloh or on Mount Zion, and David could not have aspired to the priesthood since he belonged to the tribe of Judah, not the tribe of Levi. So we must interpret the language figuratively as a noble longing to enjoy unbroken communion with God, in order to worship His glory and discern His will. Compare Psalm 23:5,6 for a similar reference to the house of God.

It was through such a life of abiding in God that David knew he would be delivered. *In the day of trouble* God would protect him, as a tent gives the traveler shelter from the sun or a high rock safety from the floods (verses 5,6). For such deliverance he will praise God in His Tabernacle (literally this time) with sacrifices and *shouts of joy* (verse 6).

Crying to God (verses 8-16)
Suddenly everything is different. The main verbs change from the third person to the second and from a statement to a prayer. The mood alters too, as confident affirmation gives

Sunset over the Sea of Galilee. "The Lord is my light and my salvation — whom shall I fear?"

place to an anxious supplication to God. So abrupt and complete is the change that some commentators have ascribed the two halves of the Psalm to different authors, or, if to the same author, at least to different occasions and circumstances. Yet those who know something of the soul's moods, of the ebb and flow of faith, and of the alternating rhythm of praise and prayer, will see no necessity for this double ascription.

David prays, seeking not only God's ear, but His face (verses 7,8). He is encouraged to do so because of God's own invitation. When God says: *Seek my face* (see margin), his heart responds: *Your face, LORD, I will seek.* True prayer is never a presumptuous approach to God, but rather a response to His gracious initiative. It is this assurance which prompts David to add: *Do not hide your face from me* (verse 9). Although he seems to recognise that his sins deserve only God's displeasure, he is sure that God, who has been his help in the past, will not now cast him off (verse 10). Even were his own parents to forsake him, he says, *the Lord will receive me* (verse 10), or "adopt me as his child," as one commentator puts it. For the likeness of God's love in the Old Testament to the tender care of a father or mother see Psalm 103:13; Isaiah 49:15; 63:16.

The negative prayer not to be forsaken is now followed by a positive petition for guidance, that his steps may be directed on to a level path. He desires to be taught God's way (verse 13), lest he be delivered into the will of his adversaries (verse 14).

The psalm ends as it began with an expression of serene confidence. The author has come through his tunnel of darkness. His faith has been sorely tried, but now it triumphs; *I am still confident of this: I will see the goodness of the LORD in the land of the living* (verse 15). He who ardently desired to see with the eye of faith the beauty of the Lord (verse 4) is sure that, before he dies, he will see the same Lord's goodness displayed in his own circumstances. So certain is he of this that he urges others to *wait for the LORD* (verse 14), that is, to trust patiently in Him. It is not enough to urge people to *be strong* and *take heart* (verse 14). These would be empty sentiments unless they are both prefaced and followed by the other injunction to *wait for the LORD*. Courage can be no more than a Stoic virtue. It is only Christian when it is the fruit of a quiet confidence in God.

Psalm 29

The Voice of the Lord

A violent thunderstorm causes most people spasms of fear.
Not so the Hebrew psalmist, who sees it rather as a manifestation of the glory of God. So convinced is he that God is in control of the elements, that he resorts to a bold anthropomorph-
ism and calls the thunder *the voice of the Lord*. We must not
imagine that he wants us to take him literally, any more than
in other psalms, where the wind is His "breath," the heavens
the work of His "fingers," and the animals feed from His open
"hand" (see for example Psalms 147:18; 8:3 and 104:28).
These are dramatic figures of speech for His immanent activity
in the world.

[1]Ascribe to the LORD, O mighty ones,
  ascribe to the LORD glory and
    strength.
[2]Ascribe to the LORD the glory due to his
    name;
  worship the LORD in the splendour of
    his holiness.

[3]The voice of the LORD is over the
    waters;
  the God of glory thunders,
  the LORD thunders over the mighty
    waters.

[4]The voice of the LORD is powerful;
  the voice of the LORD is majestic.
[5]The voice of the LORD breaks the
    cedars;
  the LORD breaks in pieces the
    cedars of Lebanon.
[6]He makes Lebanon skip like a calf,
  Sirion like a young wild ox.
[7]The voice of the Lord strikes
  with flashes of lightning.
[8]The voice of the LORD shakes the
    desert;
  The LORD shakes the Desert of
    Kadesh.

[9]The voice of the LORD twists the oaks
  and strips the forests bare.
  And in his temple all cry, "Glory!"

[10]The LORD sits enthroned over the flood;
  the LORD is enthroned as King for
    ever.
[11]The LORD gives strength to his people;
  the LORD blesses his people with
    peace.

Mount Hermon, the highest peak in Israel. Snow-capped for most of the year, the mountain reaches over 9,000 feet (2,800 metres).

The voice of the Lord

The poet seems to be describing the course of a thunderstorm as it comes from the north of Palestine (Lebanon and Sirion, or Mount Hermon, verses 5,6) and passes overhead to vent its fury upon the *Desert of Kadesh* in the far south (verse 8). Seven times *the voice of the LORD* is mentioned. One writer compares it to "successive peals of thunder," which reverberate over the countryside. At first it is heard *over the waters* (verse 3), which seems to mean "above the rainclouds," *powerful and majestic*

(verse 4). But then the thunder comes closer, and the storm brings havoc in its train, breaking down the mighty *cedars of Lebanon*, and making the mountain itself shake till it seems to *skip like a calf... like a young wild ox* (verse 6). The peals of thunder are accompanied by flashes of forked lightning (verse 7). The deer give premature birth to their young (see margin), and the forests are stripped bare by the hurricane (verse 9). So evident is the presence of God that the earth seems like His *temple*. Awestruck by His majesty, all cry *Glory!*

The glory of the Lord

This is one of several nature psalms. But it would be a grave mistake to suppose that the psalmist's intention is merely to give a poetic description of the beauties of nature. His world view is essentially God-centred. He is interested in sun and stars (Psalms 8,19), thunder and lightning (Psalm 29), birds and beasts (Psalm 104), only because they speak to him of the greatness and the goodness of God. In Psalm 29 this is plain from the introduction and the conclusion.

The introduction (verses 1,2) is a summons to the *mighty ones* to ascribe sovereignty to God. These "mighty ones" are angels, as is plain from Psalm 89:6 and Job 1:6; 2:1; 38:7. They *ascribe to the LORD the glory due to his name* (verse 2). He is *the God of glory*, and His glory is partly manifest in the solemn magnificence of a thunderstorm.

If the introduction exhorts the angels in heaven to worship God, the conclusion is a prayer that this same God will bless His people on earth. His power to do so is undoubted, for He sits enthroned *over the flood* and reigns as *king for ever* (verse 10). The transition from the description of the thunderstorm to the blessing of the people is important, because it shows that the Jews were aware of no dichotomy between nature and grace. The God of the thunder was the God of Israel, sovereign over the elements as over the affairs of men and nations. The sanctuary was not only in Jerusalem, for the forest and the wilderness were his temple, in which he could be worshiped. A thunderstorm was not an alien phenomenon. Had not Jehovah revealed Himself to His covenant people at Mount Sinai in thunder and lightning (Exodus 19:16; 20:18)? Yet He, whose voice is heard in the thunder, can also pacify the storm, making Himself known in the still small voice as well as in the earthquake (1 Kings 19:11,12). He is thus able to give to His people not only *strength* but *peace* (verse 10).

Psalm 32

The Forgiveness and Guidance of God

The last two verses of this psalm form a good introduction to it. They contain the familiar, uncompromising biblical contrast between the *wicked* and the *righteous,* the believer and the unbeliever. The particular difference between them mentioned here is that, whereas *the woes of the wicked* are many, the righteous can *rejoice in the Lord and be glad.* It is further made clear that the ground of the joy of believers is that God's *unfailing love surrounds* them. Human joy arises from God's love, and the rest of the psalm unfolds its outworking in His forgiveness and guidance of the sinner.

God's forgiveness of the past (verses 1-8)

The psalm begins with two Old Testament beatitudes, affirming the blessedness not now of the person whose delight is in God's law (verses 1,2), but of the person whose sins are forgiven. First, the facts of sin and forgiveness are described, in each case by three expressions. Wrong-doing is *transgression,* indicating a positive offence, a trespass, the stepping over a known boundary; and *sin,* a negative missing of the mark, an omission, the failure to attain an ideal; and "iniquity" (Revised Standard Version), that inward moral perversity or corruption of nature which we call "original sin."

Forgiveness is threefold too. The Hebrew word translated *forgiven* in verse 1 apparently means to remove or to lift. Sin is also *covered,* put out of sight; and therefore the Lord refuses to

¹Blessed is he
  whose transgressions are forgiven,
  whose sins are covered.
²Blessed is the man
  whose sin the Lord does not count
    against him
  and in whose spirit is no deceit.

³When I kept silent,
  my bones wasted away
  through my groaning all day long.
⁴For day and night
  your hand was heavy upon me;
my strength was sapped
  as in the heat of summer.   *Selah*

⁵Then I acknowledged my sin to you
  and did not cover up my iniquity.
I said, "I will confess
  my transgressions to the Lord" –
and you forgave
  the guilt of my sin.   *Selah*

⁶Therefore let everyone who is godly
    pray to you
  while you may be found;
surely when the mighty waters rise,
  they will not reach him.
⁷You are my hiding place;
  you will protect me from trouble
  and surround me with songs of
    deliverance.   *Selah*

⁸I will instruct you and teach
  you in the way you should go;
  I will counsel you and watch over
    you.
⁹Do not be like the horse or the mule,
  which have no understanding
but must be controlled by bit and bridle
  or they will not come to you.
¹⁰Many are the woes of the wicked,
  but the Lord's unfailing love
  surrounds the man who trusts in him.

¹¹Rejoice in the Lord and be glad, you
  righteous;
  sing, all you who are upright in heart!

A moment of meditation beside the Sea of Galilee. Every year thousands of Christian visitors find inspiration by the shores of this beautiful lake.

reckon it against the sinner. Forgiveness is thus regarded as the lifting of a burden, the covering of an ugly sight, and the cancelling of a debt. It is these verses which the apostle Paul quoted in Romans 4:6-8 as an Old Testament example of God's justification of the sinner by His grace through faith, altogether apart from works.

From this general statement of the blessedness of being forgiven, David turns to a description from personal experience of the misery of refusing to confess sin. He has written of the person *in whose spirit is no deceit* (verse 2), but now he depicts the painful consequences of deceit.

The reference is probably to his shameful dealings with Bathsheba, since, after committing adultery with her and murdering her husband, it was almost a year before he was brought to repentance by the ministry of the prophet Nathan (2 Samuel 11). During this period, while he tried to deceive himself and God, he had no peace. Indeed, long before the term "psychosomatic medicine" was coined, David tells how remorse and a tortured conscience resulted in alarming physical symptoms (verses 3,4). But at last he gave in, acknowledged his sin to God and found peace through forgiveness (verse 5).

David's vivid experience of forgiveness through repentance and confession leads him to urge others to do what he did and so receive what he received. Humble prayer to God, at a time when He may be found, always brings relief (verse 6). Moreover, David resolves constantly to do the same himself (verse 7). He has learned his lesson; he will not make the same mistake again.

45

The Church of the Beatitudes, on the northern shore of the Sea of Galilee. The church is built on the traditional site of Jesus's Sermon on the Mount.

God's guidance for the future (verses 8,9)

David's expression of confidence in God to preserve him (verse 8) is immediately answered. God gives him a promise of personal guidance, for in His steadfast love He is concerned not only to forgive the past but also to direct the future. God's guidance, like His forgivenesss, is expressed in four verbs: *I will instruct you and teach you in the way you should go; I will counsel you and watch over you* (verse 8). The picture seems to be of a mother teaching her child to walk. She never takes her eye off the child. Our God is just as tender and loving toward His people.

Nevertheless, it is important to see that verse 9 follows verse 8. God's promise of guidance is not intended to save us the bother of using our own intelligence. So to His promise he adds the command: *Do not be like the horse or the mule, which have no understanding but must be controlled by bit and bridle.* The sensitive horse and the stubborn mule have to be controlled and guided by pressure, even by force, because they are irrational animals. But we have been given a mind; we must not expect God to use a bit and bridle in His handling of us. He will treat us like human beings, not mules.

Blessed indeed are those who are surrounded by the steadfast love of God, forgiving their sins when they confess them to Him, and guiding their footsteps when they trust His promises and obey His command to use their mind.

Psalm 34

Boasting in God

One of the notable features of this psalm is its combination of worship and witness. In answer to prayer the psalmist has been marvellously delivered by God from some great peril, and his gratitude brims over now in praise, now in exhortation to others to taste and see the Lord's goodness for themselves. He describes himself as "boasting in the Lord" (verse 2). That is, he ascribes his salvation to the Lord, and because he does so out loud, those who hear him will give the glory to God too. C.H.Spurgeon, the great Baptist preacher, said: "The first ten verses are a hymn, and the last twelve a sermon."

A personal experience (verses 1-10)
The author is determined that his praise shall be not only continuous (verse 1) but congregational (verses 2,3). Since it is *in the Lord* alone (emphatic) that his soul boasts, he knows that *the afflicted* will *hear and rejoice*, for this is the only kind of boasting which makes the humble glad. So he invites them to glorify the Lord with him (verse 3), as later he urges them to look to the Lord themselves and become *radiant* (verse 5).

The reason for his worship, and his summons to others to worship, is some particular and personal experience in which he cried to God and was delivered from all his fears (verse 4)

¹I will extol the Lord at all times;
  his praise will always be on my lips.
²My soul will boast in the Lord;
  let the afflicted hear and rejoice.
³Glorify the Lord with me;
  let us exalt his name together.

⁴I sought the Lord, and he answered me;
  he delivered me from all my fears.
⁵Those who look to him are radiant;
  their faces are never covered with shame.
⁶This poor man called, and the Lord heard him;
  he saved him out of all his troubles.
⁷The angel of the Lord encamps around those who fear him,
  and he delivers them.
⁸Taste and see that the Lord is good;
  blessed is the man who takes refuge in him.

⁹Fear the Lord, you his saints,
  for those who fear him lack nothing.
¹⁰The lions may grow weak and hungry,
  but those who seek the Lord lack no good thing.

¹¹Come, my children, listen to me;
  I will teach you the fear of the Lord.
¹²Whoever of you loves life
  and desires to see many good days,
¹³keep your tongue from evil
  and your lips from speaking lies.
¹⁴Turn from evil and do good;
  seek peace and pursue it.
¹⁵The eyes of the Lord are on the righteous
  and his ears are attentive to their cry;
¹⁶the face of the Lord is against those who do evil,
  to cut off the memory of them from the earth.

¹⁷The righteous cry out, and the Lord hears them;
  he delivers them from all their troubles.
¹⁸The Lord is close to the brokenhearted
  and saves those who are crushed in spirit.

¹⁹A righteous man may have many troubles,
  but the Lord delivers him from them all;
²⁰he protects all his bones,
  not one of them will be broken.

²¹Evil will slay the wicked;
  the foes of the righteous will be condemned.
²²The Lord redeems his servants;
  no-one who takes refuge in him will be condemned.

and all his troubles (verse 6). He is evidently himself the *poor man* of verse 6. What the situation was out of which God delivered him the psalmist does not tell us.

Whatever the nature of the psalmist's distress, out of which he has been rescued, he is confident that God can do for others what He has done for him. *The angel of the LORD* (an Old Testament expression which often seems to indicate the presence of God Himself) encircles those who fear Him, as an army camps round a city to protect and deliver it (verse 7). So sure of this is the psalmist, that he appeals to others to *taste and see* for themselves and to *fear the LORD*, since those who fear Him *lack nothing* (verses 8,9). Even the *lions*, singled out as "the strongest beasts of prey, most capable of providing for themselves", sometimes go hungry, but God's trusting people will *lack no good thing* (verse 10).

The repeated references to "fear" in these verses are noteworthy. Deliverance from their fears (verse 4) is promised to those who fear the Lord (verses 7,9). This truth is neatly expressed in Tate and Brady's popular hymn paraphrasing this psalm, "Through All the Changing Scenes of Life:"

> *Fear him, you saints, and you will then*
> *have nothing else to fear;*
> *his service shall be your delight,*
> *your needs shall be his care.*

To fear God is not, of course, to be frightened of Him. Its meaning here is plain from its equivalents, namely, to "seek" Him (verse 4), to "call" to Him (verse 6) and "take refuge" in Him (verse 8), acknowledging our helplessness and looking to Him for deliverance (compare Luke 1:50).

A general instruction (verses 11-22)

The psalmist's particular deliverance through the fear of the Lord leads him to a general instruction based upon his experience. Like the Preacher in the early chapters of the Book of Proverbs, he summons his pupils to gather round him, and chooses an appropriate theme (verse 11). If they desire *many good days* (verse 12), their fear of God must express itself not just in faith, but in works, that is, in moral behavior. No one can claim to fear God who does not depart from evil (compare Job 1:1; Proverbs 16:6) both in word (verse 13) and in deed (verse 14). Nor is it enough to turn away from evil; we must positively *do good* and patiently pursue peace (verse 14).

Verses 15 to 18 describe the blessings which are granted to *the righteous*, that is, to those who fear God, shun evil, and do good. God's eyes and ears are directed toward them, while His face is turned away from the wicked (verses 15,16). He hears and delivers the righteous, draws near to the *brokenhearted*, and saves the *crushed in spirit* (verses 17,18).

On Good Friday Christians of every denomination follow the traditional route that Jesus took through the streets of Jerusalem on the way to the cross.

This does not mean that the righteous are exempt from trouble. On the contrary, *a righteous man may have many troubles* (verse 19). Nevertheless, God limits the afflictions of his people both in their duration and in their extent. He delivers them out of their trials (verse 19) and, although they are often sorely wounded, He does not allow their bones to be broken (verse 20), which seems to be a figure of speech for utter destruction (see also Micah 3:3). In Paul's language, "We are hard pressed on every side, but not crushed" (2 Corinthians 4:8).

To the unbeliever who asserts that this claim is contradicted in experience, we can only reply that, stated as a principle of God's surveillance over His people, it is true. Moreover, the differentiation between the fate of the wicked and the destiny of the righteous will finally be manifest by divine judgment in eternity. The wicked *will be condemned*; but *no-one who takes refuge in Him will be condemned* (verses 21,22).

Psalm 40

Out of the Horrible Pit

Every Christian believer is fortified in present trial by the memory of past blessings. Because we have experienced God's faithfulness in former days we are encouraged to trust Him still. Such is the theme of this psalm, which begins with a graphic description of deliverance and ends with an urgent plea for continued mercy.

An account of past deliverance (verses 1-10)
The psalmist was down a *slimy pit*, full of *mud and mire*. There is no need to suppose that this was literally his plight, like Jeremiah, whose enemies let him down by ropes into a cistern until he sank into the slime (Jeremiah 38:1-13). The pit and the bog no doubt symbolise some desolate experience of sin or depression or disease. In his helplessness, unable himself to climb out, he *waited patiently for the LORD*, and the following verses emphasise, stage by stage, the mighty deliverance of God who first heard his cry, then stooped down and drew him out of the mud, then set his feet securely upon rock, and finally

¹I waited patiently for the LORD;
  he turned to me and heard my cry.

²He lifted me out of the slimy pit,
  out of the mud and mire;
he set my feet on a rock
  and gave me a firm place to stand.
³He put a new song in my mouth,
  a hymn of praise to our God.
Many will see and fear
  and put their trust in the LORD.

⁴Blessed is the man
  who makes the LORD his trust,
who does not look to the proud,
  to those who turn aside to false gods.
⁵Many, O LORD my God,
  are the wonders you have done.
The things you planned for us
  no-one can recount to you;
were I to speak and tell of them
  they would be too many to declare.

⁶Sacrifice and offering you did not desire,
  but my ears you have pierced;
burnt offerings and sin offerings
  you did not require.

⁷Then I said, "Here I am, I have come –
  it is written about me in the scroll.
⁸To do your will, O my God, is my desire;
  your law is within my heart."

⁹I proclaim righteousness in the great assembly;
  I do not seal my lips,
  as you know, O LORD.
¹⁰I do not hide your righteousness in my heart;
  I speak of your faithfulness and salvation.
I do not conceal your love and your truth
  from the great assembly.

¹¹Do not withhold your mercy from me, O LORD;
  may your love and your truth always protect me.

¹²For troubles without number surround me;
  my sins have overtaken me, and I cannot see.
They are more than the hairs of my head,
  and my heart fails within me.

¹³Be pleased, O LORD, to save me;
  O LORD, come quickly to help me.
¹⁴May all who seek to take my life
  be put to shame and confusion;
may all who desire my ruin
  be turned back in disgrace.
¹⁵May those who say to me, "Aha! Aha!"
  be appalled at their own shame.
¹⁶But may all who seek you
  rejoice and be glad in you;
may those who love your salvation
  always say,
  "The LORD be exalted!"

¹⁷Yet I am poor and needy;
  may the LORD think of me.
You are my help and my deliverer;
  O my God, do not delay.

A young Arab boy in the so-called Tombs of the Prophets on the Mount of Olives, Jerusalem.

put a fresh song of praise in his mouth, leading many to believe (verses 1-3).

Such an experience of salvation has several fruitful consequences, notably worship (verses 4-6), obedience (verses 7-9), and witness (verses 10-12). His worship is expressed both in exclaiming how blessed the believer is (verse 4) and how numberless are the deeds and thoughts of God (verse 5).

But true worship goes beyond verbal exclamations. It is more even than the offering of sacrifices. It involves the offering of ourselves in a life of moral obedience. (For the precedence of obedience over sacrifice see 1 Samuel 15:22; Isaiah 1:10-17; Jeremiah 7:21-26; Hosea 6:6; Micah 6:6-8). This obedience is demanded *in the scroll*, that is, the written law. It begins in our *ears*, which God has *pierced*, or literally (verse 6) "dug," so that He has enabled us to hear and grasp His will.

51

But God in grace does more even than this. If He has written His law in a book, that we may know it, and whispered it into our ears, that we may understand it, He also inscribes it in our hearts, so that we "delight to do it" (verse 8, *Revised Standard Version*). This statement of knowing, loving and doing God's will, which is partially true of all His children, found its perfect fulfilment in His incarnate Son, to whom it is applied in Hebrews 10:5-9.

Salvation provokes within us, however, more than a Godward response of spiritual worship and moral obedience; it teaches us also to care for our fellows, that they too may hear of God's grace. So the psalmist asserts repeatedly that he has not concealed God's *love and... truth* (that is, faithfulness) *from the great assembly* but has publicly declared it (verses 9-10). When God sets our feet on the rock and puts His law in our ears and in our hearts, we cannot keep our lips from making His goodness known.

A prayer for present help (verses 11-17)
As in Psalm 27, the mood changes abruptly in the middle from affirmation to supplication, from a rehearsal of God's *love and... truth* to a plea that they will always preserve him. For again the psalmist finds himself in peril and distress. *Troubles without number* have encompassed him, and this time he does not leave us in ignorance of their nature: *my sins have overtaken me and I cannot see.* Indeed, they are not only too strong for him to conquer, but too many for him to count. His heart fails him (verse 12), and in self-despair he cries to God to deliver him (verse 13).

The psalm ends with a contrast between two different kinds of "seeker," those who *seek to take my life* and those *who seek you*, in a word, the godly and the ungodly. The ungodly betray their ungodliness in their persecution of the godly, and three times the psalmist prays for their overthrow (verses 14,15). But for those who instead seek God and love His salvation he desires a different destiny, namely that they may have cause from their experience to say continually "*The* LORD *be exalted!*" (verse 16). Among such he numbers himself. Left to himself, he knows he is *poor and needy*, but the Lord, who has been his deliverer, cares for him still and will yet deliver him again (verse 17).

Psalms 42, 43

The Causes and Cure of Spiritual Depression

The subject of this psalm (for Psalms 42 and 43 seem clearly to belong together) is spiritual depression, its causes and cure. The author's soul is *downcast* (verse 5), and *disturbed* within him. This is an experience by no means rare, even among godly people. Christian biographies supply many examples. Moreover, it is almost certain that our Lord Himself was alluding to these verses when He cried both "Now my heart is troubled" and "My soul is overwhelmed with sorrow" (John 12:27; Mark 14:34).

What is particularly moving is that the psalmist does not acquiesce in his condition, but three times, in words which form a refrain, he questions himself about his despondency and summons himself to trust in God (42:6,7,14,15 and 43:5, 6).

So the psalm forms three stanzas. Each begins with the psalmist's grief, in which he addresses God or his readers, and ends with the refrain, in which he addresses himself.

Psalm 42

¹As the deer pants for streams of water,
  so my soul pants for you, O God.
²My soul thirsts for God, for the living
  God.
When can I go and meet with God?
³My tears have been my
  food day and night,
while men say to me all day long,
  "Where is your God?"
⁴These things I remember
  as I pour out my soul:
how I used to go with the multitude,
  leading the procession to the house
    of God,
with shouts of joy and thanksgiving
  among the festive throng.

⁵Why are you downcast, O my soul?
  Why so disturbed within me?
Put your hope in God,
  for I will yet praise him,
    my Saviour and ⁶my God.

My soul is downcast within me;
  therefore I will remember you
from the land of the Jordan,
  the heights of Hermon – from Mount
    Mizar.

⁷Deep calls to deep
  in the roar of your waterfalls;
all your waves and breakers
  have swept over me.
⁸By day the LORD directs his love,
  at night his song is with me –
    a prayer to the God of my life.

⁹I say to God my Rock,
  "Why have you forgotten me?
Why must I go about mourning,
  oppressed by the enemy?"
¹⁰My bones suffer mortal agony
  as my foes taunt me,
saying to me all day long,
  "Where is your God?"

¹¹Why are you downcast, O my soul?
  Why so disturbed within me?
Put your hope in God,
  for I will yet praise him,
    my Saviour and my God.

Psalm 43

¹Vindicate me, O God,
  and plead my cause against an
    ungodly nation;
rescue me from deceitful and wicked
  men.
²You are God my stronghold.
  Why have you rejected me?
Why must I go about mourning,
  oppressed by the enemy?
³Send forth your light and your truth,
  let them guide me;
let them bring me to your holy
  mountain,
  to the place where you dwell.
⁴Then will I go to the altar of God,
  to God, my joy and my delight.
I will praise you with the harp,
  O God, my God.

⁵Why are you downcast, O my soul?
  Why so disturbed within me?
Put your hope in God,
  for I will yet praise him,
    my Saviour and my God.

The causes of spiritual depression

At first the author portrays himself not as cast down, but as thirsty. He thirsts for God, as a *deer* thirsts for water when overtaken by hunters or by drought. In C.S.Lewis's phrase, he has a keen "appetite for God." This is natural and right. It is, or should be, the experience of every believer. Though indeed God "satisfies the thirsty and fills the hungry with good things" (Psalm 107:9; compare Psalm 36:8,9), yet our hunger and thirst for Him are satisfied only to break out again more fiercely (compare Psalm 63:1,2).

In this case, however, the author's thirst is aggravated by two factors, which he immediately mentions. The first is

The barren wilderness of the Judean Hills; the Dead Sea can be seen in the distance.

expressed in the form of a question: *When can I go and meet with God?* (verse 2). This is what the Israelite was required to do three times a year, visiting Jerusalem for the major festivals (see Exodus 23:17), and this evidently the psalmist was unable to do. Secondly, his daily diet was one of tears because men were constantly taunting him: *Where is your God?* (verse 3). These, then, were the causes of his depression of soul: the absence of God to comfort him and the presence of men who mocked him. Each stanza reverts to this double theme.

His sense of estrangement from God is due to his enforced separation from the Temple and its worship. He writes from northern Palestine. *Mount Mizar* (verse 6) has not been identified, but is evidently a hill in the Hermon range. From this distant hill he thinks of God's *holy mountain* (43:3) and longs to be there again. Wistfully he remembers the sheer joy of worship in former days (verse 4).

As Psalm 42 is entitled *"A Maskil* (meaning perhaps 'an instruction') *of the Sons of Korah,"* it has been suggested that the author may have been one of the Korahites, men descended from Korah (Levi's great-grandson), who were gatekeepers, watchers, and musicians in the Temple (1 Chronicles 6:22-48; 9:17-32; 2 Chronicles 20:19). Certainly he writes here of praising the Lord with his voice and his harp (42:11; 43:4). But he cannot do so now because he is in exile. Instead of the Temple music he is deafened by the thunder of waterfalls and of mountain torrents in spate, as *deep calls to deep,* echoing across the valley. They seem to symbolise his calamities; he calls them God's *waves and breakers,* which have *swept over* him (verse 7). He longs to take part again in the Temple worship by day and by night (verse 9).

So, in the third stanza, he prays that God will send out His light and His truth, which like guides in the desert will lead him safely back to God's hill, dwelling, and altar, so that there again he may encounter and worship the God of his joy and gladness (43:3,4). These sentiments need not be pressed into meaning that he supposed the Temple to be the only meeting place of the soul with God — for much of the psalm is itself addressed to God while he is in exile; what he ardently desires is a renewal of that special communion with God which he had experienced in public worship on the great festivals.

The second cause of his depression is the scoffing of the heathen who kept asking incredulously: *Where is your God?* (verses 3,10). It is partly that they were idolaters, serving gods they could see and touch, while *the living God* was invisible (verse 2, compare Psalm 115:2); and partly that God appeared as inactive as He was invisible, and did not immediately vindicate His people when they were oppressed by their enemies (compare Psalm 79:10). The psalmist feels forgotten (verse 9). His spirit is so sensitive that the sharp pain of the scoffers' taunts seems like a mortal wound in his body (verse 10). He prays for vindication and deliverance (43:1).

It is, then, this combination of circumstances which has brought the psalmist to depression, and even to despair: people ridicule him for his faith in the living God, while the living God whom they mock seems indifferent and far away.

The cure for spiritual depression
Each stanza, in which the author describes his sorrowful plight, concludes with the same splendid refrain (42:5,11; 43:5). It is remarkable to note how the author speaks to himself. He will not give in to his moods. He takes himself in hand and reproaches himself for his depression. He recognises that his soul is weighed down as by a crushing burden, and inwardly *disturbed* like the raging of the sea (Psalm 46:3). But

"As the deer pants for streams of water, so my soul pants for you, O God."

why? he asks himself. Within his repeated self-questioning is an implied rebuke. Instead of answering his own questions, or excusing himself, he immediately prescribes his remedy: he must trust or "hope" in God. He must give up his introspection and self-pity, his wistful reminiscences and his pained resentment at the mockery of his enemies.

The cure for depression is neither to look in at our grief, nor back to our past, nor round at our problems, but away and up to the living God. He is our help and our God, and if we trust Him now, we shall soon have cause to praise Him again. Thus, as one writer sums up, "faith rebukes despondency and hope triumphs over despair".

Why restless, why cast down, my soul?
 Hope still, and you shall sing
The praise of him who is your God,
 Your health's eternal spring.
(Tate and Brady, 1696)

Opposite: "The God of
Jacob is our fortress". The
Citadel, Jerusalem; a
Turkish stronghold, built
on the site of Herod the
Great's palace.

Psalm 46

Immanuel, God With Us

The name of Martin Luther will always be associated with this psalm. His famous hymn *"Ein' feste Burg ist unser Gott"* is a free paraphrase of it. He and Philip Melanchthon would sing it together in times of dark discouragement, and Thomas Carlyle has made it familiar to English readers by his translation "A Safe Stronghold our God is still." It is a sublime expression of quiet confidence in God's sovereignty amid the upheavals of nature and history.

The original context was evidently some notable deliverance of Jerusalem from the attack of heathen invaders. *The city of God* (verse 4) was favored with several such deliverances. But the situation envisaged in the psalm, together with its resemblance in metaphor and phrase to some of Isaiah's prophecies, suggest the overthrow of Sennacherib's army in 701 B.C..

Although Hezekiah was King of Judah, he was a vassal of Sennacherib and was obliged to pay tribute to him. When he rebelled, the mighty army of the Assyrians came sweeping west and south like the irresistible waves of the sea. Jerusalem was soon surrounded. Sennacherib boasted that he had shut up Hezekiah "like a caged bird" and demanded his surrender.

The situation was critical. Twenty years previously Sennacherib's predecessor had taken by storm the northern capital of Samaria and depopulated the land of Israel. It looked as if Judah was to suffer the same fate. Hezekiah appealed to the prophet Isaiah, who spoke to him the word of the Lord: "Do not be afraid... for I will defend this city to save it." Suddenly and dramatically, as the secular historian Herodotus bore witness, God intervened. "That night the angel of the Lord went

¹God is our refuge and strength,
  an ever present help in trouble.
²Therefore we will not fear, though the
    earth give way
  and the mountains fall into the heart
    of the sea,
³though its waters roar and foam
  and the mountains quake with their
    surging.   *Selah*

⁴There is a river whose streams make
    glad the city of God,
  the holy place where the Most High
    dwells.

⁵God is within her, she will not fall;
  God will help her at break of day.
⁶Nations are in uproar, kingdoms fall;
  he lifts his voice, the earth melts.

⁷The LORD Almighty is with us;
  the God of Jacob is our fortress.
                    Selah

⁸Come and see the works of the LORD,
  the desolations he has brought on
    the earth.

⁹He makes wars cease to the ends of
    the earth;
  he breaks the bow and shatters the
    spear,
  he burns the shields with fire.
¹⁰"Be still, and know that I am God;
  I will be exalted among the nations,
  I will be exalted in the earth."

¹¹The LORD Almighty is with us;
  the God of Jacob is our fortress.
                    Selah

out and put to death a hundred and eighty-five thousand men in the Assyrian camp. When the people got up early the next morning – there were all the dead bodies!" So Sennacherib withdrew. See 2 Kings 18 and 19.

The psalm is in three parts, expressing first a general confidence in the power and providence of God, then a particular experience of it in the deliverance of the city, and lastly an assurance that He will establish His universal kingdom of peace. The second and third stanzas are followed by the refrain: *The* Lord *Almighty is with us; the God of Jacob is our fortress* (verses 7,11). The demands of symmetry suggest that the same refrain originally concluded the first stanza also. It is not only a statement of God's protection, but that He who is our fortress is both the powerful Lord *Almighty* and the faithful *God of Jacob*, who is bound to His people in a solemn covenant.

A general confidence (verses 1-3)
The psalmist affirms that *God is our refuge and strength* and *an ever present help in trouble*. It is this confidence which enables him to add almost with defiance: *Therefore we will not fear*. Even the worst convulsions of nature – earthquake, storm, and tempest – which strike terror into the hearts of defenseless people, will not make us afraid (verses 2,3).

A special experience (verses 4-7)
In contrast to the sea whose waters *roar and foam* (verse 3), the psalmist now mentions other and calmer waters, those of *a river whose streams make glad the city of God* (verse 4). The original reference must be to the waters of Siloam, whose gentle flowing Isaiah used as a picture of the quiet, beneficent providence of God (Isaiah 8:6). The symbol reappears in the visions of both Ezekiel (Ezekiel 47:1-12) and John (Revelation 22:1-5).

Under God's gracious rule His city is made glad (verse 4) and simply cannot *fall* because *God is within her* to protect and help her (verse 5). Let the nations "roar" like the sea and kingdoms "quake" like mountains (the same verbs are used in verse 6 as in verses 2 and 3), yet God has only to speak and *the earth melts* before Him. That is, before the voice of the Lord, the Assyrian army was scattered.

A final assurance (verses 8-11)
The writer now summons the people to take note of God's decisive intervention in the protection of Jerusalem and the *desolation* of her foes (verse 8). This divine deliverance is seen as a pledge and foretaste of the day when God will finally overthrow all warmongers and establish His kingdom of peace: *he*

Arabs plow their smallholding in the traditional manner in rocky fields near the town of Bethlehem.

breaks the bow and shatters the spear, he burns the shields with fire (verse 9). The vision recalls the prophecies of Isaiah about the beating of swords into ploughshares and spears into pruninghooks, and the using of military boots and bloodstained garments as fuel for the fire (Isaiah 2:4; 9:5).

No sooner has this promise of peace been given than God Himself, its guarantor, is heard to speak: *Be still, and know that I am God.* It was His voice which overthrew the Assyrians (verse 6); it is His voice which pacifies His people. He is God for ever and is already here and now (probably a present tense) exalted in the earth (verse 10). This majestic affirmation prompts His people to respond in the refrain: *The LORD Almighty is with us.* Again, the words have an Isaianic ring, reminding us of his great prophecy about Immanuel, "God with us" (Isaiah 7:14; 8:8,10).

We also live in an epoch of crisis. The old order has gone. The social revolution begun 150 years ago continues and grows in pace. We hear wars and rumors of wars. People's hearts fail them for fear. Can we say: "We will not fear"? Indeed we can; but only if we believe the other affirmations of this psalm: *I am God* and *The LORD Almighty is with us.* As John Wesley said with his dying breath: "The best of all is, God is with us."

Psalm 51

Divine Mercy for the Penitent

Psalm 46 sets forth the sovereignty of God; this psalm extols His mercy. Though He is exalted among the nations (Psalm 46:10), He does not despise the broken and contrite heart of the penitent (51:17).

This fourth of the seven so-called "penitential psalms" refers in its title to David's grievous sin. From his palace roof one spring afternoon, he saw a beautiful woman named Bathsheba, desired her for himself, and committed adultery with her. He had her husband, Uriah the Hittite, sent into the hottest part of the battle with the Ammonites, where he would certainly be killed and, in fact, was killed. David then proceeded to take her as his wife. Only when the prophet Nathan was sent by God to rebuke him, did he feel his guilt, confess his sin, and plead for mercy. His simple "I have sinned against the LORD" in 2 Samuel 12:13 is here elaborated into such a prayer for God's mercy in cleansing and renewal as has been the language of penitents ever since.

The need of God's mercy

We can appreciate our need of divine mercy only when we have seen the gravity of our sin. As in Psalm 32, so in verses 1 and 2 of this psalm, three separate Hebrew words are used to describe David's offence, namely *transgression* (the crossing of

¹Have mercy on me, O God,
  according to your unfailing love;
  according to your great compassion
  blot out my transgressions.
²Wash away all my iniquity
  and cleanse me from my sin.

³For I know my transgressions,
  and my sin is always before me.
⁴Against you, you only, have I sinned
  and done what is evil in your sight,
  so that you are proved right when you
    speak
  and justified when you judge.
⁵Surely I have been a sinner from birth,
  sinful from the time my mother
    conceived me.
⁶Surely you desire truth in the inner
    parts;
  you teach me wisdom in the inmost
    place.

⁷Cleanse me with hyssop, and I shall be
    clean;
  wash me, and I shall be whiter than
    snow.
⁸Let me hear joy and gladness;
  let the bones you have crushed
    rejoice.
⁹Hide your face from my sins
  and blot out all my iniquity.

¹⁰Create in me a pure heart, O God,
  and renew a steadfast spirit within
    me.
¹¹Do not cast me from your presence
  or take your Holy Spirit from me.
¹²Restore to me the joy of your salvation
  and grant me a willing spirit, to
    sustain me.

¹³Then I will teach transgressors your
    ways,
  and sinners will turn back to you.

¹⁴Save me from bloodguiltiness, O God,
  the God who saves me,
  and my tongue will sing of your
    righteousness.
¹⁵O Lord, open my lips,
  and my mouth will declare your
    praise.
¹⁶You do not delight in sacrifice, or I
    would bring it;
  you do not take pleasure in burnt
    offerings.
¹⁷The sacrifices of God are a broken
    spirit;
  a broken and contrite heart,
  O God, you will not despise.

¹⁸In your good pleasure make Zion
    prosper;
  build up the walls of Jerusalem.
¹⁹Then there will be righteous sacrifices,
  whole burnt offerings to delight you;
  then bulls will be offered on your
    altar.

a boundary), *sin* (the missing of a mark), and *iniquity* (depravity of nature). The thought behind these words is unfolded in an important recognition of the essence and origin of sin.

The essence of sin is revolt against God: *Against you, you only, have I sinned and done what is evil in your sight, so that you are proved right when you speak and justified when you judge* (verse 4). It is true that David had sinned against Bathsheba and Uriah, against his family and nation, but first and foremost, he had offended against the love and law of God. He had coveted, stolen, committed adultery and murder and, in so doing, had broken four of the five last commandments and brought himself under the just sentence of God. Compare Romans 3:4 where Paul quotes these words to establish the unswerving justice of God in His dealings with human beings. It is because we are under the judgment of God that we need the mercy of God.

If the essence of sin is rebellion, its origin is in our fallen nature: *Surely I was sinful at birth, sinful from the time my mother conceived me* (verse 5). This does not, of course, mean that the marvellous processes of conception and birth are in themselves sinful, but that our human nature from its first beginnings has been infected with sin. As we inherit it from our parents, it is twisted with self-centredness. This is "original sin," and David came to recognise it when his sinful passions of lust, jealousy, cruelty, and avarice overcame and overthrew him.

It is when we see ourselves as we are, on the one hand rebels against God and under the judgment of God, and on the other prisoners of a corrupt nature, that we come, like David, to despair of ourselves and to cry to God for mercy.

The expression of God's mercy

The mercy of God expresses itself in meeting the sinner's need, giving him both pardon and purity.

In praying for pardon, David uses two vivid metaphors. First, he asks God to *blot out* his transgressions (verses 1,9). The verb denotes the removal of writing from a book (see for example Exodus 32:32). He seems to think of his sins as a list of offences of which he is accused or a catalogue of debts which he cannot pay. He pleads that the entry be erased.

Secondly, he acknowledges that his sins have defiled him and prays that God will *wash* and *cleanse* him (verse 2), until his black stains are removed and he becomes *whiter than snow* (verse 7). Since in certain Old Testament rituals a bunch of hyssop was dipped in blood or water, which was then ceremonially sprinkled, the word *hyssop* is used in verse 7 as a symbol of cleansing.

But David knew his need of purity as well as pardon. God

Opposite: Good Friday in
Jerusalem. "Have mercy
on me, O God, according
to your unfailing love;
according to your great
compassion blot out my
transgressions".

demanded *truth in the inner parts* (verse 6); yet David's very
nature was corrupt (verse 5). Only the creative power of God
could make him a new person. So he prayed: *Create in me a
pure heart, O God, and renew a steadfast spirit within me*
(verse 10). He longed, that is, for a new nature with new and
pure desires, and for a spirit both *steadfast* (verse 10) and *willing* (verse 12). He seems to have known too, before the full
New Testament revelation had been given, that such a new
nature and spirit could be imparted to him only by the Holy
Spirit Himself (verse 12).

If God in mercy would grant him both a clean conscience
and a clean heart, the sorrow which his sin had caused would
be turned into *joy and gladness* (verse 8, compare verse 12).

The results of God's mercy
The last part of the psalm (verses 13-19) is devoted to the
results which follow an experience of the cleansing and
recreating mercy of God. David resolves that his attitude both
to other people and to God will be different.

First, he accepts his responsibility to his fellow humans. He
has sinned against them; now he will serve them in a new way.
When his own transgressions have been forgiven, he will *teach
transgressors* God's way, so that they return to Him (verse 13).
He prays to be delivered from *bloodguilt* (verse 14). Perhaps he
means that, although he has indeed been guilty of the blood of
Uriah, he is determined that God shall not require at his hand
the blood of sinners whom he has failed to warn and teach
(compare Ezekiel 3:16-27 and 33:1-20).

His second responsibility is toward God. He will use his lips
in worship as well as witness: *O Lord, open my lips, and my
mouth will declare your praise* (verse 15). It is this that God
desires, not *sacrifice* or *burnt offerings*. He does not mean that
no sacrifice at all is pleasing to God, but that the kind of sacrifice He chiefly desires, especially from a transgressor like
David, is *a broken and contrite heart*. And then, when he is forgiven, he may offer the further sacrifice of praise and
thanksgiving (verse 15; compare Psalm 50:14,23).

The last two verses have seemed to many commentators not
to belong to David's psalm at all. There is an apparent reference to the rebuilding of Jerusalem's walls in verse 18,
although the words could be figurative. And verse 19 (*burnt
offerings to delight you*) seems to contradict verse 16 (*you do
not take pleasure in burnt offerings*). The discrepancy is only
superficial, however, and is consistent with much teaching in
both psalms and prophets. This is not that sacrifices are not
acceptable to God in themselves, but that they please Him only
if they are expressive of a contrite, worshiping heart and an
obedient will.

64

Opposite: An Arab
woman cuts grain with a
traditional sickle in fields
in the West Bank region.
"The land will yield its
harvest, and God, our
God, will bless us."

Psalm 67

Saving Health to the Nations

This psalm appears to be greatly concerned about the blessing
of God. Three times in its brief seven verses it reverts to this
theme, now in prayer that God may bless us, and now in affirmation that He will do so.

This gives the psalm a rather homely touch, because we ourselves frequently talk about the blessing of God. "God bless
you," we say as we bid someone good-bye, or as we end a letter. We even utter the same prayer when people sneeze! We
seem so anxious to secure the divine blessing for our friends,
that we lose no opportunity of expressing our desire for it.

Now what do we mean when we seek God's blessing? The
language of this psalm is rather beautiful because it is bor-
rowed from the words of the high priest's blessing. First given
by God to Moses, for use by Aaron and his sons in the Tabernacle worship, it is recorded in Numbers 6:24-26, "The LORD
bless you and keep you; the LORD make his face to shine upon
you and be gracious to you; the LORD turn his face towards you
and give you peace." This blessing came to be used regularly in
the Temple services at Jerusalem, and is still a favorite in Christian worship today. Echoes of it are heard in several psalms
(for instance Psalm 4:6; 29:11; 31:16; 80:3,7,55). So here
some words from the ancient blessing of Aaron form the
groundwork of this psalm, which was no doubt composed for
liturgical use in the Temple.

When read as a whole, Psalm 67 teaches us that there is some
justification for praying for ourselves, that there are unselfish
reasons for praying the selfish prayer *God bless us*. Two such
motives are given – immediate and ultimate.

¹May God be gracious to us and bless
     us
and make his face to shine upon us;
                              Selah
²may your ways be known on earth,
     your salvation among all nations.

³May the peoples praise you, O God;
     may all the peoples praise you.
⁴May the nations be glad and sing for
     joy,
for you rule the peoples justly
and guide the nations of the earth.
                              Selah

⁵May the peoples praise you, O God;
     may all the peoples praise you.

⁶Then the land will yield its harvest,
     and God, our God, will bless us.
⁷God will bless us,
     and all the ends of the earth will fear
     him.

The knowledge of God

The first reason why we desire that God shall bless us is in order that through us His salvation may be known to all humankind (verses 1,2). In that case Israel's motive in seeking God's blessing was not selfish after all. They prayed that God would bless them, not in order to wallow comfortably in His blessing themselves, but in order that it might pass from them to others. They longed that God would be merciful to them, that thereby the nations might receive His mercy, and come to know His ways and saving health.

We need to remember that Israel made very audacious claims for herself and her God. She claimed to be the special people of God, with whom He had entered into an everlasting covenant. She poked fun at the dead, dumb idols of the nations. She affirmed that her God was the only living, active and true God. So of course her heathen neighbors were watching her, now quizzically, now incredulously. They wanted some evidence to support Israel's contention. "Where is now your God?" they asked. They wanted to know what God could do for His people; what difference He made to them; whether the claims of Israel had any substance to them.

That is why Israel prayed *God be gracious to us and bless us.* If only Aaron's blessing would come true! If only God's mercy were granted to them! If only God were specially to bless them, and the light of His smile were to be upon them and with them always! Surely then the nations would see for themselves? Then the nations would have visual proof of the existence, activity and grace of God? Then the nations would come to know His way and His salvation, and experience themselves that God rules righteously and leads His people like a shepherd (verse 4).

The same principle operates today. Non-Christian people are watching us. We claim to know, to love and to follow Jesus Christ. We say that he is our Savior, our Lord, and our Friend. "What difference does he make to these Christians?" the world asks searchingly. "Where is their God?" It may be said without fear of contradiction that the greatest hindrance to evangelism in the world today is the failure of the church to supply evidence in her own life and work of the saving power of God. Rightly may we pray for ourselves that we may have God's blessing and mercy and the light of His countenance — not that we may then monopolize His grace and bask in the sunshine of His favor, but that others may see in us His blessing and His beauty, and be drawn to Him through us.

The worship of God

Verses 3-5 form another refrain in this psalm. They give the second reason why we desire God's blessing. It is not just in

68

order that others may come to know Him. For why do we want them to know God? Just for their own benefit? Just that they may receive His salvation? Are we wanting others to do what we have renounced ourselves? We are not asking God's blessing for our selfish ends; are we content that others should receive His blessing for theirs? That hardly makes sense.

We need to look beyond the salvation of the nations to its ultimate purpose, which is that they too should come to worship and praise God. We should desire their salvation not just that they shall know Him for themselves, but that they shall praise Him for Himself. The greatest incentive in all evangelism is not the need of human beings but the glory of God; not that they shall receive salvation, but that they shall give to God the honor that is due to His name, acknowledging and adoring Him for ever. We cannot be content until every convert has become a worshiper.

A monk sweeps the gardens of the lakeside Galilee church which commemorates the appearance of the risen Christ to the apostles. It was on that occasion that He instructed Peter: "Feed my lambs."

Psalm 73

The Prosperity of the Wicked

The providence of God, His moral ordering of the world, is a problem which has always baffled the human mind. The book of Job and Psalms 37 and 49 as well as 73 are devoted to this theme. The problem can be simply stated. God has revealed Himself as good and just, punishing wickedness and rewarding goodness. If He is all-powerful as well as all-good, why does He allow such a morally perverse state of affairs to continue on earth? Far from justice catching up on the wicked, they flourish "like a green tree" (Psalm 37:35). They not only get away with their wickedness but seem to be exempt from the troubles which befall other people. In a word, honesty is not the best policy. It does not pay to be good. It is the wicked who prosper, while adversity overtakes the righteous. Such is the background to this psalm.

The problem (verses 1-14)
The psalmist begins with the conviction held by all godly people, even in the face of apparently contradictory circumstances: *Surely God is good... to those who are pure in heart* (verse 1). This is an axiom of revealed religion and cannot on any account be surrendered. *But as for me,* he immediately continues, *my feet had almost slipped; I had nearly lost my foothold. For I envied* the arrogant when I saw the prosperity of the wicked (verses 2,3). First, he was troubled by their immunity to disease and disaster (verses 4,5). Next, by their arrogance (verses 6-9). Their eyes and heart, their talk and looks (verses 7,8) are full of conceit. Not only do *their tongues take possession of the earth* (verse 9), but they even *lay claim to heaven* (verse 9). Added to their immunity to trouble and their arrogant ways is their popularity with the world (verses 10,11). The people ask why God, if indeed He knows about them, does not punish them (verse 11).

The psalmist concludes his description of the wicked: *always carefree, they increase in wealth.* Then he cries out bitterly: *Surely in vain have I kept my heart pure* (verse 13), for while the wicked flourish, *all day long I have been plagued* (verse 14). If the wicked prosper, it is vain to be righteous. Righteousness does not pay; the big dividends go to the wicked.

¹Surely God is good to Israel,
   to those who are pure in heart.

²But as for me, my feet had almost
      slipped;
   I had nearly lost my foothold.
³For I envied the arrogant
   when I saw the prosperity of the
      wicked.

⁴They have no struggles;
   their bodies are healthy and strong.
⁵They are free from the burdens
      common to man;
   they are not plagued by human ills.
⁶Therefore pride is their necklace;
   they clothe themselves with
      violence.
⁷From their callous hearts comes
      iniquity;
   the evil conceits of their minds know
      no limits.
⁸They scoff, and speak with malice;
   in their arrogance they threaten
      oppression.
⁹Their mouths lay claim to heaven,
   and their tongues take possession
      of the earth.

¹⁰Therefore their people turn to them
   and drink up waters in abundance.
¹¹They say, "How can God know?
   Does the Most High have
      knowledge?"

¹²This is what the wicked are like –
   always carefree, they increase in
      wealth.
¹³Surely in vain have I kept my heart
      pure;
   in vain have I washed my hands in
      innocence.
¹⁴All day long I have been plagued;
   I have been punished every
      morning.

¹⁵If I had said, "I will speak thus,"
   I would have betrayed your children.
¹⁶When I tried to understand all this,
   it was oppressive to me
¹⁷till I entered the sanctuary of God;
   then I understood their final destiny.

¹⁸Surely you place them on slippery
      ground;
   you cast them down to ruin.
¹⁹How suddenly are they destroyed,
   completely swept away by terrors!

²⁰As a dream when one awakes,
   so when you arise, O Lord,
   you will despise them as fantasies.

²¹When my heart was grieved
   and my spirit embittered,
²²I was senseless and ignorant;
   I was a brute beast before you.
²³Yet I am always with you;
   you hold me by my right hand.
²⁴You guide me with your counsel,
   and afterwards you will take me into
      glory.
²⁵Whom have I in heaven but you?
   And earth has nothing I desire
      besides you.
²⁶My flesh and my heart may fail,
   but God is the strength of my heart
   and my portion for ever.

²⁷Those who are far from you will perish;
   you destroy all who are unfaithful to
      you.
²⁸But as for me, it is good to be near God.
   I have made the Sovereign LORD my
      refuge;
   I will tell of all your deeds.

The right approach to the problem (verses 15,16)
The reason why the psalmist so nearly stumbled and fell (verse
2) is that his approach was wrong. He made at least three mis-
takes. First, he *envied* the wicked (verse 3). But it is always
wrong to envy the sinner's liberty to sin. "Do not let your heart
envy sinners, but always be zealous for the fear of the LORD"
(Proverbs 23:17). Secondly, he became bitter against God, as
he later confesses (verses 21-22). To make presumptuous com-
plaints against God is to behave like an ignorant animal, not
like a rational human being. Thirdly, he was tempted to give
up. When he tried to understand, he says, *it was oppressive to
me* (verse 16). He could find no solution and was inclined to
give in to despair.

But perplexity and hopelessness lasted only *till I entered the
sanctuary of God* (verse 17). Perception is granted to those
who humbly seek God's face. The Christian in the twentieth
century needs to learn this lesson. When we are perplexed by
the problems of God's providential rule in the world, we are
neither to look at the wicked with envy nor at ourselves in bitter self-pity. Nor should we give up looking for any solution
and lapse into despair, but rather fall on our knees and look at
God. Then "from the secret place of the Most High we see
things as God sees them" (Campbell Morgan).

The solution (verses 17-27)

Our problems are aggravated because we are narrow-minded and short-sighted. It is a question of perspective. A mountain which appears menacing when we stand at its foot and it towers above us, shrinks into harmless insignificance when we view it from a distance or from the air. So the problem of God's providence cannot be solved in the limited context of time and earth; its solution awaits the next world and eternity. Many of life's inequalities will remain now. But wrongs will be righted, evil avenged, and good vindicated in the final judgment. This is why we need to keep going into *the sanctuary of God*; it is there that our perspective is adjusted and our vision clarified.

What the psalmist was able in God's sanctuary to grasp was the *final destiny* of these people (verse 17). They flourish now, it is true, but God sets them *on slippery ground*. In the words of Jesus, they are on "the broad road that leads to destruction." Ultimately death will claim them and they will be *destroyed.* Indeed, *as a dream when one awakes*, the very memory of them will vanish away (verses 17-19).

If that is the fate of the wicked, very different is the destiny of the righteous: *I am always with you* (verse 23). That is, though the ungodly flourish now, only to perish in the end, the godly enjoy the presence of God perpetually, both now and forever (verse 24). God's people may suffer want and persecution, but their abiding wealth is in God Himself. In one of the sublimest expressions of personal religion in the Old Testament the psalmist continues: *Whom have I in heaven but you? And earth has nothing I desire besides you* (verse 25). In heaven and earth, in time and eternity, the living God is his *portion for ever* (verse 26). Such communion with God is eternal life; death can neither disturb nor destroy it.

In conclusion, verses 27 and 28 summarise the contrasting destinies of the godly and the ungodly which the psalmist perceived in the sanctuary of God: *Those who are far from you will perish... but as for me, it is good to be near God.* No doubt nearness to God does not appear "good" to the materialist, since it may involve sorrow and suffering in the world. But those who prize true riches know that our real and eternal "good" is in God.

Psalm 84

The Courts of the Lord

The Temple in Jerusalem was for the Jew the most sacred spot on earth, for there in the Holy of Holies was the Shekinah glory, the visible manifestation of the presence of God. Of course the pious Israelite knew perfectly well, as Solomon had said, that God does not "dwell on earth" and that "the heaven, even the highest heaven cannot contain" Him (1 Kings 8:27). Nevertheless, He had been pleased to "put his name" in Jerusalem and to cause the symbol of His presence to appear upon the mercy-seat behind the veil of the Temple. As a result, every Israelite loved the Temple and looked forward eagerly to every chance to visit it, especially on the three annual festivals. He could sincerely sing: *How lovely is your dwelling-place, O Lord Almighty* (verse 1). The same longing for the Temple is found in Psalms 42 and 43 and in some of the pilgrim psalms (120-134).

The blessedness of others (verses 1-7)
The psalmist begins by expressing how desirable God's dwelling-place is to Him. His whole being longs for it, *soul, heart,* and *flesh*. He *yearns, even faints* for it, because to enter *the courts of the Lord* is equivalent to approaching *the living God* Himself. But for some reason he is prevented from fulfilling his heart's desire. So he looks with envy upon those, both birds and humans, who can enjoy what at present is denied to him.

¹How lovely is your dwelling-place,
 O Lord Almighty!
²My soul yearns, even faints
  for the courts of the Lord;
 my heart and my flesh cry out
  for the living God.

³Even the sparrow has found a home,
  and the swallow a nest for herself,
  where she may have her young –
 a place near your altar,
  O Lord Almighty, my King and my
   God.
⁴Blessed are those who dwell in your
   house;
  they are ever praising you. *Selah*

⁵Blessed are those whose strength is in
   you,
 who have set their hearts on
  pilgrimage.
⁶As they pass through the Valley of
   Baca,
  they make it a place of springs;
 the autumn rains also cover it with
  pools.
⁷They go from strength to strength
 till each appears before God in Zion.

⁸Hear my prayer, O Lord God Almighty;
 listen to me, O God of Jacob. *Selah*
⁹Look upon our shield, O God;
 look with favour on your anointed
  one.

¹⁰Better is one day in your courts
  than a thousand elsewhere;
 I would rather be a doorkeeper in the
  house of my God
 than dwell in the tents of the wicked.
¹¹For the Lord God is a sun and shield;
  the Lord bestows favour and
   honour;
 no good thing does he withhold
  from those whose walk is blameless.

¹²O Lord Almighty,
  blessed is the man who trusts in you.

Opposite: The Dome of
the Rock, Jerusalem,
which is built on the site of
the Jewish Temple, for the
Jews the most sacred spot
on earth.

He thinks of the sparrows, the most numerous and common birds in the world, constructing their nests in every available nook and cranny of the Temple buildings. The *swallow* is probably the swift. Large numbers still visit Palestine on migration, and many nest even today in the precincts of the Mosque of Omar in Jerusalem. How fortunate these birds seem to the psalmist! They are permitted to dwell in the immediate proximity of the altars of God. Chattering sparrows and screaming swifts appear to unite with the people of God as they worship him. To them the writer now turns, the priests who *dwell* in God's house, always praising him (verse 4), and the pilgrims who visit it from time to time. He pronounces them both *blessed* (verses 4,5).

He concentrates on the pilgrims (verses 5-7), no doubt because he longs to be one himself, and gives a graphic description of their journey up to Jerusalem. They *have set their hearts on pilgrimage* (verse 5), and their resolute purpose strengthens them on their arduous trek. He pictures them passing through an arid valley (*the Valley of Baca*). But even such forbidding parts of the journey do not deter the pilgrims. On the contrary, they find there a *place of springs* for *the autumn rains also cover it with pools*. In other words, "hope sustains them at every step" (Bishop Perowne). They go *from strength to strength*, fortified by the joyful expectation of appearing before God in Zion (verse 7).

A personal prayer (verses 8-12)
As the psalmist describes the blessedness of sparrows and swifts, pilgrims and priests, who visit the Temple or dwell there, his own longing to join them breaks out into a prayer: *O LORD God Almighty, listen to me...* (verse 8). There follows a prayer for God's *anointed one* (verse 9), which must mean the king. We can only guess its relevance in this context. Perhaps it is that the nation's welfare was bound up in the king's.

The writer goes on to indicate the reason for his prayer to visit the Temple, and expresses it forcefully in terms of both time and space (verse 10). One day in the courts of the Lord, he says, is to him better *than a thousand elsewhere*, while to be a mere *doorkeeper in the house of my God*, approaching only the threshold of the Temple, was preferable to dwelling at ease *in the tents of the wicked*. Only a day. Only a doorkeeper. And yet such a fleeting and distant contact with God would be satisfying, since He is a *sun*, bathing us with light, *and shield*, defending us from evil. More than that, He gives *favour and honour*; in fact *no good thing does he withhold from those whose walk is blameless* (verse 11).

The psalm ends with another statement of who is *blessed*. It is not only the priests who dwell in the Temple precincts (verse

4) and the pilgrims who visit them (verse 5), but all people who put their trust in God (verse 12), whether or not they have the opportunity to go up to Jerusalem.

Christian worshipers have no difficulty in applying this psalm to themselves, for the New Testament tells us plainly what the temple of God is which we may call *lovely* and make the object of our desire. First, it is the church, not only universal (Ephesians 2:21) but local (1 Corinthians 3:16; 2 Corinthians 6:16), that is, every company of believers. God does not dwell in temples made with hands (Acts 7:48) but among His people. We do not need to travel to Jerusalem to meet Him. When only two or three of us have met in the name of Christ, He is there in our midst (Matthew 18:20). This is why we love to come together for public worship.

But the final fulfilment of the temple idea will be heaven, the new Jerusalem, of which it is written: "I did not see a temple in the city, because the Lord God Almighty and the Lamb are its temple," and "Now the dwelling of God is with men, and he will live with them. They will be his people, and God himself will be with them and be their God" (Revelation 21:22,3). In this sense, too, Christian believers know in their own experience the psalmist's ardent longing for the temple of God. We thirst for God, and our Christian hope sustains us on our weary pilgrimage to heaven.

In his paraphrase of this psalm, Henry Francis Lyte skilfully combines the double New Testament application of the temple theme to Christian worship and to heaven:

> *Pleasant are your courts above,*
> *In the land of light and love;*
> *Pleasant are your courts below,*
> *In this land of sin and woe.*
> *Oh! my spirit longs and faints*
> *For the converse of your saints,*
> *For the brightness of your face,*
> *For your fulness, God of grace.*

Psalm 90

Life's Transient Dream

This psalm sets out the brevity of human existence in the light of God's eternity. The author refers to some period of special affliction (verse 15) as well as to humankind's universal frailty and sinfulness. Yet he betrays no sign of despair or complaint; his spirit is one of humble submission and trust.

God's eternity (verses 1-6)
The psalm opens with a magnificent statement of the eternity of God, because of which He has ever been the *dwelling-place* of His people. The word for *dwelling-place* is the same as that in Deuteronomy 33:27: "The eternal God is your *refuge*, and underneath are the everlasting arms." Amid all the ups and downs of life our only security is in Him who, before the birth of the mountains and creation of the earth, indeed *from everlasting to everlasting*, is God.

Human beings are by contrast creatures of dust. In a clear allusion to Genesis 3:19, God is described as commanding them to return to dust (verse 3). Such is the reality of death, "earth to earth, ashes to ashes, dust to dust." We are not only mortal, but extremely short-lived. To God a whole millennium is equivalent to a day (compare 2 Peter 3:8) or even to one of the watches of the night (verse 4). But in comparison with the

¹Lord, you have been our
    dwelling-place
  throughout all generations.
²Before the mountains were born
    or you brought forth the earth and
    the world,
  from everlasting to everlasting you
    are God.

³You turn men back to dust,
    saying, "Return to dust, O sons of
    men."
⁴For a thousand years in your sight
    are like a day that has just gone by,
    or like a watch in the night.
⁵You sweep men away in the sleep of
    death;
  they are like the new grass of the
    morning –
⁶though in the morning it springs up
    new,
  by evening it is dry and withered.

⁷We are consumed by your anger
    and terrified by your indignation.
⁸You have set our iniquities before you,
    our secret sins in the light of your
    presence.
⁹All our days pass away under your
    wrath;
  we finish our years with a moan.
¹⁰The length of our days is seventy years –
    or eighty, if we have the strength;
  yet their span is but trouble and sorrow,
    for they quickly pass, and we fly
    away.
¹¹Who knows the power of your anger?
    For your wrath is as great as the fear
    that is due you.
¹²Teach us to number our days aright,
    that we may gain a heart of wisdom.

¹³Relent, O LORD! How long will it be?
    Have compassion on your servants.

¹⁴Satisfy us in the morning with your
    unfailing love,
  that we may sing for joy and be glad
    all our days.
¹⁵Make us glad for as many days as you
    have afflicted us,
  for as many years as we have seen
    trouble.
¹⁶May your deeds be shown to your
    servants,
  your splendour to their children.

¹⁷May the favour of the Lord our God rest
    upon us;
  establish the work of our hands for
    us –
  yes, establish the work of our hands.

Opposite: "Satisfy us in
the morning with your
unfailing love, that we
may sing for joy and be
glad all our days."

divine timelessness, our human life is *like the new grass*, which
flourishes in the morning but is withered by the evening,
scorched by sun and wind. This is a constant theme of Scripture, and other vivid metaphors are used to stress the brevity of
our life on earth. It is like water spilt on the ground, like a
shadow which passes when the sun comes out, and like smoke
or mist dispersed by the wind.

God's wrath (verses 7-11)

In the next paragraph the thought moves on from God's eternity to His wrath. At first it may seem an abrupt transition, but
the psalmist sees human mortality against the dark
background of God's displeasure at sin. This is not only that
the nation was passing through some calamity which he attributes to the judgment of God, but because he recognises that
death is the penalty for human sin (Genesis 2:17; 3:19;
Romans 5:12). So he writes of our *iniquities* and even *our secret sins* being open before God (verse 8), and says that *all our
days pass away under your wrath* (verse 9). Our average span
of life may be seventy years, yet even these are *trouble and sorrow*. This is not said in bitterness, but in calm and sober
realism. Every human being is destined to die, and our brief life
span is spent under the judgment of God (verse 11), unless and
until we find mercy. This brings us naturally to the prayers
with which the psalm concludes.

God's mercy (verses 12-17)

The first prayer inspired by a sense of human sin and mortality
is in verse 12: *Teach us to number our days aright, that we may
gain a heart of wisdom. Wisdom* consists of knowing and fear-
ing God; life is so short that it is folly to ignore Him. The rich
farmer in the parable of Jesus, who planned and spoke as if life
lasted for ever, God called a fool.

Secondly, *Satisfy us in the morning with your unfailing love*,
for if we find our peace in the love of God early, we shall *be
glad all our days* (verses 13,14). Further, the joy God gives us
will make up for the years of adversity (verse 15).

The third prayer is concerned with our *work*. One of the
tragedies of death is that it interrupts our labor and cuts short
our achievement. This is true, however, only of human
endeavor undertaken in human strength. When God shows *his
work* to His servants, manifesting his power on their behalf
and blessing them with His favor, the result is that He prospers
the work of our hands for us (verses 16,17). The only work
which lasts is that which God establishes.

The brevity of life should still constrain us to get a heart of
wisdom, namely to make God our refuge, to find rest in His
love and fruitful labor under His blessing.

Psalm 91

The Defence of the Most High

This psalm has an unusual distinction: it is the only passage of Scripture which (at least in the sacred record) is quoted by the devil! (See Matthew 4:6 and Luke 4:10,11.) This is more important than it sounds, because actually the devil misquoted it, or rather misapplied it. He urged the Son of God to throw Himself down from the pinnacle of the Temple and trust God's promise (verses 11 and 12) that His angels would protect Him, so that He would not hurt Himself. The devil is not the only person who has attempted to misapply Psalm 91, as if it promised an unconditional security in any and every circumstance.

Our Lord knew, however, that to jump from the roof of the Temple on the basis of this psalm's promise of divine protection would be to tempt God. Only children of God who are living in the will of God can expect the protection of God. Even then, they have no guarantee of being shielded from all harm (see verse 15). What they know is that ultimately, whatever their circumstances may be, they are secure in God's love. Psalm 91 is, in fact, the Old Testament equivalent of Romans 8:31-39.

The best way to grasp the sequence of thought is to see that first the believer speaks to God (verses 1,2); then the psalmist addresses the believer (verses 3-13); while finally God intervenes, speaking to the reader, and Himself confirms the believer's assurance of security which is the theme of the psalm (verses 14-16).

¹He who dwells in the shelter of the Most High
will rest in the shadow of the Almighty.
²I will say of the LORD, "He is my refuge and my fortress,
my God, in whom I trust."

³Surely he will save you from the fowler's snare
and from the deadly pestilence.
⁴He will cover you with feathers,
and under his wings you will find refuge;
his faithfulness will be your shield and rampart.
⁵You will not fear the terror of night,
nor the arrow that flies by day,

⁶nor the pestilence that stalks in the darkness,
nor the plague that destroys at midday.
⁷A thousand may fall at your side,
ten thousand at your right hand,
but it will not come near you.
⁸You will only observe with your eyes
and see the punishment of the wicked.

⁹If you make the Most High your dwelling –
even the LORD, who is my refuge –
¹⁰then no harm will befall you,
no disaster will come near your tent.
¹¹For he will command his angels concerning you
to guard you in all your ways;

¹²they will lift you up in their hands,
so that you will not strike your foot against a stone.
¹³You will tread upon the lion and the cobra;
you will trample the great lion and the serpent.

¹⁴"Because he loves me," says the LORD, "I will rescue him;
I will protect him, for he acknowledges my name.
¹⁵He will call upon me, and I will answer him;
I will be with him in trouble,
I will deliver him and honour him.
¹⁶With long life will I satisfy him
and show him my salvation."

The believer (verses 1,2)

The believer's faith is grounded upon who God is. He is *the Most High* and *the Almighty* on the one hand (verse 1), infinite in transcendence and power; but on the other he is *the Lord* (verse 2), Yahweh, the covenant God of Israel, bound to His people by a solemn undertaking. To *rest in the shadow* of such a God is wisdom; He is the believer's *refuge* and *fortress*.

The Church of the Holy Sepulchre, Jerusalem. This much-visited church is believed to be built over the site of Golgotha, where Jesus was crucified. "If you make the Most High your dwelling... then no harm will befall you."

The psalmist (verses 3-13)

Having quoted this confession of faith, the psalmist now endorses it, encouraging believers in it and assuring them of their safety. Bold imagery is used to illustrate the divine defence which is promised. God will defend them as a mother bird hides her chicks under her wings; His *faithfulness* will be to them as a soldier's *shield* (verse 4). What, then, are the perils from which believers will be delivered? They are variously described: *the fowler's snare... the deadly pestilence* (verse 3), *the terror of night... the arrow... by day* (verse 5), *the pestilence and the plague* (verse 6).

It is perfectly possible to interpret this figurative language as referring to literal calamities. But some writers suggest that real demons are in view, derived perhaps from Babylonian sources.

Be that as it may, deliverance is plainly promised from all evil. *Ten thousand* may succumb to it (verse 7), and the *wicked* shall reap the *punishment* of their sins (verse 8), but to those who make the Lord their refuge, it may be confidently asserted: *no harm will befall you* (verses 9,10). God's angels will protect them (verses 11,12; compare Psalm 34:7 and Hebrews 1:14), so that not even the *lion and the cobra... and the serpent* (verse 13) shall be able to harm them. The snake is the subtlest and the lion the strongest of all creatures. It is not without significance that Satan is called "that ancient serpent" and depicted as prowling round "like a roaring lion" (Revelation 12:9; 20:1 and 1 Peter 5:8).

The Lord (verses 14-16)

Finally, the Lord himself is heard to speak, neither to the believer nor to the psalmist, but to the reader, approving the believer's faith and the psalmist's theme. Has the psalmist affirmed: *he will save you*? He is quite right. Twice God echoes the same words Himself: *I will rescue... I will deliver* (verses 14,15). Why? *Because he loves me.* God is the supreme object of the believer's love as well as faith, and it is to those who love God that the assurance is given that "in all things God works for their good" (Romans 8:28). Not that believers can afford to be idle and do nothing. They must trust God, and express their faith in prayer. Then God *will* answer them. The divine deliverance does not, however, always mean an escape from trouble; it sometimes means finding God with them *in trouble* (verse 15). The final promise which God makes to His trusting servants is of *long life* and *salvation* (verse 16). It is not impossible that, like the prophets, the psalmist wrote more than he knew, for the ultimate meaning of security is that eternal life and salvation which are found in Jesus Christ alone.

82

Psalm 95

An Invitation to Sing and to Hear

This psalm is a summons to the people of God, who know Him as the *Rock* of their salvation (verse 1), both to sing His praises and to hear His word. From at least as early as the fourth century A.D. it has been sung in many churches at the beginning of public worship.

An invitation to sing God's praise (verses 1-7)
In King Henry VIII's devotional primer, Psalm 95 is called "a song stirring to the praise of God." And what a stirring summons it is! In verses 1, 2, and 6 there are seven exhortations one after the other. Indeed, members of the congregation, no doubt gathered in the Temple courts, are represented as engaged in mutual exhortation. They are inciting one another to worship and urging each other to sing the praises of God, since public worship is essentially congregational.

In this psalm we are given incentives as well as invitations to worship. We do not just hear the repetitive *let us*, but the added *for the LORD is...* giving us a reason for our praise. Not until we grasp who the Lord is, are we inwardly moved to worship Him.

Who, then, is He? The answer of this canticle is that He is both *the great God* (verse 3) and *our God* (verse 7).

First, He is *the great God*. He is supreme in heaven (verse 3), *the great King above all gods*. There is no need to assume that the psalmist credited them with an objective reality, for "all the

¹Come, let us sing for joy to the LORD;
   let us shout aloud to the Rock of our
      salvation.
²Let us come before him with
      thanksgiving
   and extol him with music and song.

³For the LORD is the great God,
   the great King above all gods.
⁴In his hand are the depths of the earth,
   and the mountain peaks belong to
      him.
⁵The sea is his, for he made it,
   and his hands formed the dry land.

⁶Come, let us bow down in worship,
   let us kneel before the LORD our
      Maker,

⁷for he is our God
   and we are the people of his pasture,
   the flock under his care.

Today, if you hear his voice,
⁸do not harden your hearts as you did at
      Meribah,
   as you did that day at Massah in the
      desert,
⁹where your fathers tested and tried me,
   though they had seen what I did.
¹⁰For forty years I was angry with that
      generation;
   I said, "They are a people whose
      hearts go astray,
   and they have not known my ways."
¹¹So I declared on oath in my anger,
   "They shall never enter my rest."

A squall on the Sea of Galilee. "The sea is his, for he made it, and his hands formed the dry land."

gods of the nations are idols" (Psalm 96:5). God is also supreme on earth (verses 4,5). Every dimension is included, in order to show that nothing is beyond the dominion of God. The depths of the earth, the heights of the mountains, and the broad expanses of sea and land are all His. They are *in his hand* (verse 4), because *his hands formed them* (verse 5). The hand that made the universe in the beginning still holds the universe today. God is the controller of the natural order because He was the creator of it.

Secondly, *he is our God* (verse 7). Far above us in His greatness, He is yet close to us in His goodness. His majesty is tempered with mercy, and his glory with grace. Did He make the world? He made Israel, too. He is *the LORD our Maker* (verse 6; see also Psalms 100:3; 149:2; Isaiah 51:13; 54:5). The Creator of all things is the Redeemer of His special people. He is our Shepherd as well, calling us *the people of his pasture* (verse 7).

Psalm 95 makes it plain that our mood will change in worship according to which aspect of God is occupying our attention. In verses 1 and 2 the invitation is to make a joyful noise to the Lord and come into His presence with thanksgiving, *for the LORD is a great God*. Because of his greatness in creation, we may well shout aloud in jubilation. But in verse 6 the invitation is to *kneel before the LORD*. Why? *For he is our God* (verse 7). Has this great God condescended to be our God, becoming our shepherd and calling us His sheep? Then this is no moment for exuberant hilarity, but rather for awe and wonder, as with bated breath we prostrate ourselves before Him in reverence and humility.

With the end of verse 7 the mood changes again. The speaker changes too. So far the congregation have been exhorting one another; now God intervenes and speaks to His people Himself.

An invitation to hear God's word (verses 8-11)

We are not only to open our lips to sing God's praise, but to open our ears to hear His word. It is noteworthy that those who are exhorted to hear God's voice have been described in the previous verse as *the flock under his care*, because of course a sheep should know the shepherd's voice. Compare John 10:2-4.

The early days of Israel are taken by God as a striking object lesson. A month or two after the Exodus, just before they reached Mount Sinai, the children of Israel camped at Rephidim. There was no water. So the people found fault with Moses: "Give us water to drink. Why did you bring us out of Egypt to kill us, our children and cattle with thirst?" Moses prayed to the Lord, and at His instruction struck the rock with the rod of God, and water gushed out. Moses then gave to this place two names, *Massah* meaning testing or temptation, and *Meribah* meaning quarrelling or provocation. This story is recorded in Exodus 17:1-7.

Forty years later a similar crisis arose at Kadesh. Water was again miraculously provided for the people, when they complained to Moses. This place came to be known as *Meribah-Kadesh*, to distinguish it from the *Meribah* at Rephidim. This second story is recorded in Numbers 20:1-13.

God's people had tested their God. They had put Him to the proof. Although they had seen His works, they had no faith in Him. God had wonderfully rescued them from their bondage in Egypt. He later established His covenant with them, gave them His special revelation, and provided for them in the wilderness. Yet here they were rebelling against Him, and doubting His love and goodness. No wonder we go on to read, *forty years I was angry with that generation*. God also described them as *a people whose hearts go astray* (verse 10). Their wandering in the wilderness was an outward counterpart to their straying hearts. So great was Israel's sin, unbelief, and rebellion, that it aroused a feeling of revulsion in the heart and mind of God (verse 11). God is revealed in Scripture as a God of love and wrath, of goodness and severity. He hates sin with an implacable hatred, while yet loving the sinner with an inextinguishable love.

The letter to the Hebrews makes these verses an urgent message for Christians today. "So the Holy Spirit says: 'Today, if you hear his voice, do not harden your hearts as you did in the rebellion, during the time of testing in the desert...'" (Hebrews 3:7,8). It is today which is the day of salvation; we must beware lest we become "hardened by sin's deceitfulness" (Hebrews 3:13).

Psalm 98

Jehovah, the Savior-King

The occasion of this psalm is evidently some great national victory, which has been achieved by God's right hand and holy arm, and in the sight of the nations. Whether the divine victory was over Egypt or Babylon or some other foe, it certainly foreshadows that mightier salvation from sin, Satan and death, which God has brought to us through Jesus Christ His Son. This is the most marvellous of the *marvellous things* (verse 1) which God has done, and it prompts the people of God to keep singing a *new song*, new from ever fresh wonder at His grace. Christian songs of praise are fundamentally a rejoicing in the *marvellous things* which God has done.

The psalmist's call to praise is not only due to God's mighty acts of the past. He sees them also as evidence of the present reign of God, and as a pledge that He will set up His final kingdom of righteousness on earth. His threefold theme, therefore, concerns God the Savior, the King and the Judge. He invites God's people to sing to Him as their Savior (verses 1-4), *all the earth* (verse 4) to worship Him as King (verses 4-6), and nature (sea, the world, rivers and mountains) to do homage to Him as the coming Judge (verses 7-9).

God the Savior (verses 1-3)
The victory of God which inspired the composition of this psalm was gained by Himself alone. He had no human co-operation. He relied upon *his right hand and his holy arm*

¹Sing to the LORD a new song,
　for he has done marvellous things;
his right hand and his holy arm
　have worked salvation for him.
²The LORD has made his salvation
　　known
　and revealed his righteousness to
　the nations.
³He has remembered his love
　and his faithfulness to the house of
　Israel;
all the ends of the earth have seen
　the salvation of our God.

⁴Shout for joy to the LORD, all the earth,
　burst into jubilant song with music;
⁵make music to the LORD with the harp,
　with the harp and the sound of
　singing,

⁶with trumpets and the blast of the
　ram's horn –
　shout for joy before the LORD, the
　King.

⁷Let the sea resound, and all that is in it,
　the world, and all who live in it.
⁸Let the rivers clap their hands,
　let the mountains sing together for
　joy;
⁹let them sing before the LORD,
　for he comes to judge the earth.
He will judge the world in
　righteousness
　and the peoples with equity.

A young Jewish boy reads
from the Law at his
Barmitzvah ceremony in
front of the Western Wall,
Jerusalem.

(verse 1). Since "God is spirit" (John 4:24), he has no body, of course, and therefore neither hands nor arms. Nevertheless, these vivid anthropomorphic expressions symbolise both His strength and His direct intervention on behalf of His people. The redemption from Egypt and from Babylon are alike ascribed in Scripture to the strong arm or mighty hand of God (see for example Exodus 15:6,12; Psalm 44:1-3; and Isaiah 52:10; 59:16; 63:5).

Further, this victory of God was no secret affair, but rather a public spectacle. He *revealed* it in the sight of the nations (verse 2). What they saw was His *salvation* and His *righteousness.*

God had also made known His *love and his faithfulness to the house of Israel* (verse 4). Israel were God's chosen people, with whom He had entered into a solemn covenant. This covenant He would never break, nor forget. Indeed, the recent deliverance was a proof of His loyalty to it. So Israel could praise God not only for His power, which gained the victory, but for His faithfulness out of which it sprang. Although it was a victory gained for Israel by Israel's God, (*our God*), it had been seen by *all the ends of the earth* in fulfilment of the prophecy of Isaiah 52:10, which John the Baptist applied to the salvation of Jesus (Luke 3:6). The combination of *love* and *faithfulness* may also be seen throughout Psalm 89, in Psalms 92:2 and 100:5, and Micah 7:20.

God the King (verses 4-6)

If the people of Israel have been summoned to praise God, so now are the inhabitants of *all the earth* (verse 4; compare Psalm 100:1). Even if they have not like Israel experienced His salvation, they can with Israel recognise His kingdom. He is *the Lord, the King* (verse 6). His mighty deliverance of His people is a visible token of His sovereign rule over the affairs of human beings and nations. He is to be worshiped not merely with a *shout* (verse 4), but with singing and musical instruments (verse 5,6).

It seems likely that these outward expressions of rejoicing are chosen because they commonly accompanied the accession or coronation of a new king. When Zadok anointed Solomon king, they blew the trumpet, and the people shouted and rejoiced with music (1 Kings 1:39,40). Similarly, when the boy king Joash was crowned and anointed by Jehoiada the priest, there was a clapping of hands as well (2 Kings 11:12-14). So the reign of Jehovah is to be similarly celebrated with singing and shouting, with clapping of hands and blowing of trumpets (compare Psalm 47). There was in Hebrew worship what C.S.Lewis calls a certain "gusto."

Part of the Good Friday procession of Christian pilgrims along the *Via Dolorosa*, in the old city of Jerusalem.

God the Judge (verses 7-9)

In this worship of men and women, expressed jubilantly through musical instruments and the human voice, the whole range of animate and inanimate nature is now invited to join. The sea and its denizens, the world and its inhabitants, the floods and the hills are together to be joyful *before the* LORD (verses 6,9). The roaring of the sea is its worship; in the splashing of the floods we can hear them clap their hands. The reason for their rejoicing lies yet in the future.

It seems to be recognised that nature is subject to some kind of bondage, as the apostle Paul was later to show in Romans 8:18-25, and it would be delivered only when God came to set up His kingdom. He is already King (verse 6), but the earth does not yet acknowledge His rule. So He is coming to judge the earth, and its peoples (verse 9). Only when God's rule is established on earth (as it has begun to be through Christ, although the Messianic kingdom is pictured in this psalm as a rule of Jehovah Himself), will the peoples and nature itself be subdued and righteously governed. He who has already shown His righteousness in the saving of His people (verse 2), will exhibit it again in His judging of the world. This judgment will include the punishment of the wicked, as is made plain in Isaiah 11:1-5. But even in this too we may rejoice, for we shall recognise that "true and just are his judgments," and concurring in them we shall cry, "Amen, Hallelujah!" (Revelation 19:1-5).

Psalm 100

The Lord is God and Good

This psalm was sung by the Israelites first in the Temple, and then in the daily synagogue services. The medieval church sang it in the service called Lauds. It is most popular today in its metrical version, "All people that on earth do dwell," which was probably composed by William Kethe, a sixteenth-century Scotsman and friend of the Reformer John Knox.

It has only five verses, but it is an eloquent summons to worship; and the worship to which it bids us is to have two marks.

Two characteristics of worship

This psalm is often called "the Jubilate", which means "O be joyful!" or "shout aloud!". Joy is to characterise our worship. Psalm 100 is one of a group of eight which celebrate the kingly sovereignty of Jehovah. "The LORD reigns, he is robed in majesty... Your throne was established long ago." "The LORD is the great God, the great King above all gods." "Say among the nations: 'The LORD reigns.'" "The LORD reigns, let the earth be glad." "Shout for joy before the LORD, the King." "The LORD reigns, let the nations tremble." (Psalms 93:1,2; 95:3; 96:10; 97:1; 98:6; 99:1). Of these royal psalms the hundredth is the doxology.

For if God is king, what can our worship be but joyful? Away with funereal faces and doleful dirges! Joy, gladness, and singing are to be the accompaniment of worship.

> ¹Shout for joy to the LORD, all the earth,
> ² Serve the LORD with gladness;
> come before him with joyful songs.
> ³Know that the LORD is God.
> It is he who made us, and we are his;
> we are his people, the sheep of his
> pasture.
>
> ⁴Enter his gates with thanksgiving
> and his courts with praise;
> give thanks to him and praise his
> name.
> ⁵For the LORD is good and his love
> endures for ever;
> his faithfulness continues through all
> generations.

The Golden Gate, Jerusalem, looks out across the Kidron Valley. Both Jews and Moslems believe that this will be the site of the Last Judgment.

Our worship is to be universal as well as joyful. *Shout for joy all the earth* (verse 1). It is true that this psalm concerns Jehovah, the God of Israel; but the psalmist realises that He is not Israel's monopoly. Had He not sworn to Abraham: "In your seed shall all the families of the earth be blessed"? Is it not written in Isaiah 56:6,7: "And foreigners who bind themselves to the LORD to serve him, to love the name of the LORD... these will I bring to my holy mountain and give them joy in my house of prayer... for my house will be called a house of prayer for all nations."? Then no nation should stand aside from this call to worship. Jehovah is not the tribal deity of Israel, but the sovereign Ruler over all the earth. When we assemble for worship, therefore, we should desire not only to make a joyful noise ourselves, but that all nations should unite with us in our joyful task.

The rest of this psalm is devoted to an exposition of why the nations should join us. Worship is not only to be joyful and universal, but reasonable.

The greatness of God

Know that the LORD *is God* (verse 3). How we worship depends on what we know. Knowledge and understanding play an important part in our worship. Christians do not worship "an unknown God," like the ancient Athenians, but a God who has revealed Himself.

What then are we to know? The gods of the heathen are idols; they can neither see, nor speak, nor act. Our God is a living and active God. Moreover, the chief evidence which the psalmist gives of His activity is to be found in the history of Israel. He redeemed His people from their bondage in Egypt, entered into a covenant with them at Mount Sinai, led them across the wilderness, and settled them in the Promised Land. In a word He *made* them (compare Deuteronomy 32:6,15 and Psalm 95:6). *It is he who made us, and we are his* (verse 3). Of this sovereign, intervening activity of God, two vivid illustrations are given.

First, God is the potter. *It is he who made us.* God is here likened to a craftsman. It is not the individual, but the nation, to which the phrase refers. Israel is sometimes called by God in the Old Testament "the work of my hands" (see for example Isaiah 29:23; 60:21).

With what immense skill and patience did the divine potter pursue His labor! His raw material was always unpromising, and often recalcitrant. Others would have long since abandoned all hope of success. But He persevered. Undeterred by any setback, and refusing to be discouraged by any disappointment, He went on fashioning Israel into a vessel of honor, fit for His own use.

Secondly, God is the shepherd. *We are his people, the sheep of his pasture.* The potter who made them was the shepherd who tended them. Through all the vicissitudes of their colorful career, He protected and guided them. He watched over them with all the conscientious tenderness of an eastern shepherd.

So it is with us also. God has redeemed us and brought us to Himself. We can say that He is our potter and our shepherd. Nothing could indicate more clearly and emphatically than this what we owe to the sovereign grace of God. It is He who has made us and we are His people. We have neither created nor constituted ourselves the people of God. "By the grace of God we are what we are." What we are is therefore cause for praise, not for pride.

No wonder the psalmist bursts into another call to worship: *Enter his gates with thanksgiving and his courts with praise; give thanks to him and praise his name* (verse 4). Our worship is to be joyful simply because it is grateful.

The goodness of God
The Lord is not only great, but *good* (verse 5). There is ground to praise Him not only for what He has done, but for what He is.

Wherein does His goodness consist? It consists in His love which *endures for ever* and His *faithfulness* (verse 5). Our God is a covenant-keeping God. He is neither fickle nor faithless; His word is dependable, and His promises are trustworthy. From generation to generation He remains the same. From everlasting to everlasting He is God.

We are summoned to worship Him not just because He has made us and taken us to Himself to be His own, but because He will stay by us. The heavenly potter will never discard His work; He will persist in fashioning it into a vessel that is beautiful and useful. The heavenly shepherd will never abandon His sheep; He will make them lie down in green pastures and lead them beside still waters. His goodness and mercy will follow them all the days of their life. The vessel is safe in the potter's hand. The sheep are safe in the shepherd's arms.

Psalm 103

The Benefits of God's Grace

Psalm 103 is, undoubtedly, one of the best-loved psalms, just as Henry Francis Lyte's free paraphrase, "Praise my Soul, the King of heaven," is one of the most popular hymns in the English language. We have here the authentic utterance of a redeemed child of God, who piles up words to express his gratitude to the God of grace. His praise expands in three concentric circles. First, he addresses himself and seeks to arouse himself to the proper worship of God: *Praise the LORD, O my soul* (verses 1-5). Next, he recalls the mercy of God to all the people of His covenant (verses 6-18). Finally, he summons the whole of creation to join in the chorus of praise (verses 19-22).

God's benefits to me (verses 1-5)
The first five verses of the psalm are very personal, as the author confronts himself with his duty and exhorts his own sluggish soul to worship. He desires not only to praise God's *holy name* (verse 1), acknowledging the holiness or unique "otherness" of His being, but to remember *all his benefits*. Indeed, he is determined that his worship of God shall be as total as are God's blessings to him: *all my inmost being* in response to *all his benefits*. These benefits have been given to

¹Praise the LORD, O my soul;
   all my inmost being, praise his holy name.
²Praise the LORD, O my soul,
   and forget not all his benefits.

³He forgives all my sins
   and heals all my diseases;
⁴he redeems my life from the pit
   and crowns me with love and compassion.
⁵He satisfies my desires with good things,
   so that my youth is renewed like the eagle's.

⁶The LORD works righteousness
   and justice for all the oppressed.

⁷He made known his ways to Moses,
   his deeds to the people of Israel:
⁸The LORD is compassionate and gracious,
   slow to anger, abounding in love.

⁹He will not always accuse,
   nor will he harbour his anger for ever;
¹⁰he does not treat us as our sins deserve
   or repay us according to our iniquities.
¹¹For as high as the heavens are above the earth,
   so great is his love for those who fear him;
¹²as far as the east is from the west,
   so far has he removed our transgressions from us.
¹³As a father has compassion on his children,
   so the LORD has compassion on those who fear him;
¹⁴for he knows how we are formed,
   he remembers that we are dust.
¹⁵As for man, his days are like grass,
   he flourishes like a flower of the field;
¹⁶the wind blows over it and it is gone,
   and its place remembers it no more.

¹⁷But from everlasting to everlasting
   the LORD's love is with those who fear him,
   and his righteousness with their children's children –
¹⁸with those who keep his covenant
   and remember to obey his precepts.

¹⁹The LORD has established his throne in heaven,
   and his kingdom rules over all.

²⁰Praise the LORD, you his angels,
   you mighty ones who do his bidding,
   who obey his word.
²¹Praise the LORD, all his heavenly hosts,
   you his servants who do his will.
²²Praise the LORD, all his works
   everywhere in his dominion.

   Praise the LORD, O my soul.

both body and soul, for God both *forgives all my sins* and *heals all my diseases* (verse 3). Further, He redeems my life *from the pit* (verse 4), that is the grave or Sheol. Not content with saving the psalmist from sin, disease and death, God lavishes positive blessings upon him as well. He *crowns* him (verse 4), that is, He makes His child a king (compare Psalm 8:5).

God also satisfies him *with good things* (verse 5), so that our *youth is renewed like the eagle's*. Maybe this alludes to an ancient fable that the eagle soars periodically so near to the sun that it drops scorched into the sea and emerges miraculously rejuvenated, or to the bird's annual molt and "eclipse" after the breeding season, until the plumage is renewed the following spring. Here, as in Isaiah 40:31, the eagle is used as a symbol of youth and strength.

These, then, are God's personal benefits to the psalmist. Delivered from sin, sickness, and death, he feels himself as privileged as a king and as vigorous as an eagle.

God's mercy to His people (verses 6-18)

The psalmist now changes from the singular to the plural, from the particular benefits which he has himself received to God's general grace to all the people of His covenant. Whenever they have been *oppressed* he has displayed on their behalf both *righteousness and justice* (verse 6). The most signal revelation of this was to Moses and to the children of Israel under Moses' leadership (verse 7). Such just dealing with His people was an expression of His grace.

Indeed, what the psalmist goes on to write is a kind of meditation on that glorious revelation of God's name to Moses: "The Lord, the Lord, the compassionate and gracious God, slow to anger, abounding in love and faithfulness" (Exodus 34:6). After quoting these words (verse 8), our author proceeds to enforce them by two negative statements, three illustrations and a striking contrast.

The two negatives indicate that God sets limits to his own righteous wrath against sin. The first is a time limit, that He *will not always accuse*. The second is a restraint upon the expression of His anger that, instead of that just judgment , *he does not treat us as our sins deserve* (verses 9,10). Then follow three positive illustrations of God's grace. His steadfast love is as high as heaven, His forgiveness removes our sins as far away as infinity, and His pity is as tender as a father's for his children, because He knows our human frailty (verses 11-14).

The mention of human weakness leads to the final underlining of the mercy of God, which, as in Psalm 90, takes the form of a contrast between human transience and the eternity of God's love. Humankind flourishes like grass, and perishes like grass too when the hot desert wind blows upon it; but toward

Wild flowers beside the road, near Samaria. "As for man, his days are like grass, he flourishes like a flower of the field."

those who reverence God, keep His covenant and remember His commandments, His *love* and *righteousness* endure for ever and enrich their posterity (verses 15-18). This assurance of God's unfailing love to successive generations has brought comfort to many mourners as they have stood round the grave and watched a coffin lowered to its final resting place.

God's dominion over all creation (verses 19-22)
In the last paragraph the psalmist turns from the love of the Lord for His covenant people to His sovereignty over all His creation. He has *established his throne in heaven* and from there *rules over all* (verse 19). Thus convinced of God's universal kingdom, the author summons the whole created order to praise him. First, he addresses the mighty *angels*, called also God's *hosts* and *servants*, whose characteristic activity is to *do his will* (verses 20,21). Next he turns to the lower orders of God's creation and calls on *all his works everywhere* to worship Him. Finally, he comes back to himself and concludes the psalm as he began it, with the personal exhortation: *Praise the LORD, O my soul* (verse 22).

Psalm 104

The Works of God in Nature

Psalms 103 and 104 form a perfect pair and illustrate the balance of the Bible. Both begin and end with the words *Praise the LORD, O my soul.* Psalm 103 goes on to tell of the goodness of God in salvation, Psalm 104 of the greatness of God in creation (verse 1). Psalm 103 depicts God as the father with His children, Psalm 104 as the Creator with His creatures. Psalm 103 catalogues His *benefits* (verse 2), Psalm 104 His *works* (verses 13,24,31).

The author evidently has in mind the narrative of Genesis 1 and draws his inspiration from it. He follows approximately the same order, beginning with light and ending with human beings. He describes with great poetic beauty how God made the heavens and the earth (verses 1-9), and provides drink, food and shelter for all birds and beasts (verses 10-23). After a further meditation on God's many varied works in both creating and preserving "all creatures great and small" (verses 24-30), he concludes with a prayer that God's glory may endure, a resolve to worship God throughout his life, and a desire that sinners who spoil God's world shall be no more (verses 31-35).

It is important to notice the form which the psalmist's "gusto for nature", as C.S.Lewis called it, took. He does not praise nature for its own sake; "there are no nature lyrics in the psalms. Nature is referred to only to the extent that it points to him who made everything" (C.S.Lewis). This emphasis is preserved in Sir Robert Grant's fine (if free) paraphrase, "O Worship the King" (1833).

God's creation of heaven and earth (verses 1-9)
Most of the verbs in this paragraph should probably be put in the past tense and understood to refer to the creation of the heavens (verses 1-4) and the earth (verses 5-9). We should beware of taking these verses literally. The author writes as a poet, not as a scientist. We are not intended to picture God riding on a chariot of clouds or building the earth like a house on actual, material foundations. All this is imagery.

What the passage does teach us is that God is the creator of the universe, and that He has revealed Himself in it. In His essential being He is invisible, but He makes Himself known in the visible order which He has made. The light is His garment, the heavens are His tent, the sky His chambers, and the clouds

¹Praise the LORD, O my soul.

O LORD my God, you are very great;
  you are clothed with splendour and
    majesty.
²He wraps himself in light as with a
    garment;
  he stretches out the heavens like a
    tent.
³ and lays the beams of his upper
    chambers on their waters.
He makes the clouds his chariot
  and rides on the wings of the wind.
⁴He makes winds his messengers,
  flames of fire his servants.

⁵He set the earth on its foundations;
  it can never be moved.
⁶You covered it with the deep as with a
    garment;
  the waters stood above the
    mountains.
⁷But at your rebuke the waters fled,
  at the sound of your thunder they
    took to flight;
⁸they flowed over the mountains,
  they went down into the valleys,
  to the place you assigned for them.
⁹You set a boundary they cannot cross;
  never again will they cover the earth.

¹⁰He makes springs pour water into the
    ravines;
  it flows between the mountains.
¹¹They give water to all the beasts of the
    field;
  the wild donkeys quench their thirst.
¹²The birds of the air nest by the waters;
  they sing among the branches.

¹³He waters the mountains from his
    upper chambers;
  the earth is satisfied by the fruit of his
    work.
¹⁴He makes grass grow for the cattle,
  and plants for man to cultivate –
  bringing forth food from the earth:
¹⁵wine that gladdens the heart of man,
  oil to make his face shine,
  and bread that sustains his heart.
¹⁶The trees of the LORD are well watered,
  the cedars of Lebanon that he
    planted.
¹⁷There the birds make their nests;
  the stork has its home in the pine
    trees.
¹⁸The high mountains belong to the wild
    goats;
  the crags are a refuge for the coneys.

¹⁹The moon marks off the seasons,
  and the sun knows when to go down.
²⁰You bring darkness, it becomes night,
  and all the beasts of the forest prowl.
²¹The lions roar for their prey
  and seek their food from God.
²²The sun rises, and they steal away;
  they return and lie down in their
    dens.
²³Then man goes out to his work,
  to his labour until evening.

²⁴How many are your works, O LORD!
  In wisdom you made them all;
  the earth is full of your creatures.
²⁵There is the sea, vast and spacious,
  teeming with creatures beyond
    number –

living things both large and small.
²⁶There the ships go to and fro,
  and the leviathan, which you formed
    to frolic there.

²⁷These all look to you
  to give them their food at the proper
    time.
²⁸When you give it to them,
  they gather it up;
  when you open your hand,
  they are satisfied with good things.
²⁹When you hide your face,
  they are terrified;
  when you take away their breath,
  they die and return to the dust.
³⁰When you send your Spirit,
  they are created,
  and you renew the face of the earth.

³¹May the glory of the LORD endure for
    ever;
  may the LORD rejoice in his works.
³²He looks at the earth, and it trembles;
  he touches the mountains, and they
    smoke.

³³I will sing to the LORD all my life;
  I will sing praise to my God as long
    as I live.
³⁴May my meditation be pleasing to him,
  as I rejoice in the LORD.
³⁵But may sinners vanish from the earth
  and the wicked be no more.
Praise the LORD, O my soul.

Praise the LORD.

His chariot, while He makes the winds His messengers and fire and flame His servants (verses 2-4). "In comparing the light to a robe," comments the reformer John Calvin, "he signifies that, though God is invisible, yet his glory is manifest."

Similarly, the earth is described as having been established upon firm foundations and then covered with the deep. This is the primeval chaos, when "the earth was formless and empty" and "darkness was over the surface of the deep" (Genesis 1:2). Then the separation of earth from sea is dramatically portrayed (as in Genesis 1:9,10): the waters *flowed over the mountains, they went down into the valleys, to the place you assigned for them* (verse 8).

God's provision for birds and beasts (verses 10-23)
In this part of the psalm the verbs are mostly in the present tense, and remind us that Christians are not deists. The

nineteenth-century deists believed that God had wound up the universe and set it in motion like a gigantic clockwork toy. The Bible teaches, however, that God is a living God, ceaselessly active in the control and the care of what He has made. He makes provision for the *beasts of the field* and *the birds of the air* (verses 11,12). "Ecology" would be a term too grandiosely scientific to apply to this paragraph; yet this is what the author is depicting. He is fascinated by God's marvellous adaptation of the earth's resources to the needs of living creatures, and vice versa.

Thus, the streams which flow through the valleys provide drink for the animals (verses 10,11), while God's rain waters the mountains (verse 13) and the trees (verse 16). Similarly, humans and beasts are supplied with food from the earth, including wine, oil and bread (verses 14,15). Even carnivorous lions are said to seek their food from God (verse 21).

Living creatures require more than food and drink, however; they need shelter also, to protect them from the fury of the elements and in their breeding season. So birds, which *sing among the branches* (verse 12), also *make their nests in them* (verse 17). Storks build *in the pine trees* (verse 17), while *the high mountains* are a refuge *for the wild goats* and *the crags for the coneys* (verse 18; this is also translated badger and rabbit; it is evidently a hyrax). Further safety is provided by the cover of darkness, when *all the beasts of the forest prowl.* Then, when *the sun rises... they steal away... and lie down in their dens*; whereas human beings, by contrast, work by day and sleep at night (verses 19-23).

God's creation and preservation of all creatures (verses 24-30)
The psalmist interrupts his descriptions with an outburst of praise (verse 24). Both earth and sea teem with His creatures, *living things both large and small* (verse 25). The sea is also the place of ships and the playground of Leviathan (verse 26). The latter is evidently a great sea creature, which some scholars think "is the whale, some the porpoise; in Job 41 it is probably the crocodile". Whatever Leviathan is, God is represented in the Talmud as playing with it.

Further, if God has made all creatures in His wisdom, He also cares for them in His faithfulness. They *all look to you* (verse 27). They depend upon Him for their food and breath. Not that they are inactive in feeding themselves, for they have to *gather up* their food; but God *gives* it. This truth is further enforced by striking anthropomorphisms, which speak of God's *hand* and *face* (verses 28,29). Just as we have seen a child at the zoo or in the farmyard, offering food to some animal on the palm of an outstretched hand, so God opens His hand, that His creatures may be *satisfied with good things.* But when He turns away from them and hides His face, *they are terrified*. When further, He takes away their breath, *they die and return to the dust*. When, on the other hand, He sends His Spirit (or "breath"), they are not only created in the first place, but continuously renewed.

Food and life are the basic needs of every creature, and here their presence is attributed to the open hand and quickening breath of God, their absence to His hidden face. To modern ears it all sounds very naive. Can we believe such things in this age of science and technology? We have already noted that the descriptive passages are figurative, whether in the use of poetic or of anthropomorphic imagery.

But the truth behind the figures stands. God the Creator is lord of His creation. He has not abdicated His throne. He rules what He has made. No Christian can have a mechanistic view of nature. The universe is not a machine which operates by inflexible laws, nor has God made laws to which He is himself now a slave. The very term "natural laws" is only a convenient expression for the observed consistency of God's working. He is living and active in His universe, and we depend upon Him for our "life and breath and everything else" (Acts 17:25). It is right to thank Him not only for our creation, but for our preservation as well.

In conclusion, the psalmist expresses the fervent wish that God's glory (seen in His works) may always endure, and that God may continue to rejoice in His works, as He did when they left His hand at the beginning (verse 31; compare Genesis 1:31), lest He should look upon the earth with judgment instead of favor (verse 32). The psalmist determines himself to spend his whole life praising God and hopes that this psalm, his meditation upon the works of God, may please Him (verses 33,34). Yet he recognises that there are *sinners* and *wicked* people who do not give to God, their creator and preserver, the glory that is due to His name (verse 35). The God in whose hand their breath is, they have not honored (Daniel 5:23). His earnest desire is that such sinners should no longer be permitted to deface God's good world.

The city of Jerusalem from the Mount of Olives. Jewish pilgrims at festival time would have their first glimpse of the city when they reached the top of this hill.

Psalm 121

The Lord our Keeper

The fifteen psalms from 120 to 134 inclusive form a self-contained group. At one time they were probably a separate collection. Each is entitled *A Song of Ascents*, literally, "A Song of Goings-up." The most probable meaning of this term is that these psalms were sung by groups of pilgrims while they were "ascending" toward Jerusalem for one of the three major annual festivals. Each of these psalms, then, is a pilgrimage song. They are brief, and most of them show a great love for Zion and the Temple and an ardent desire for the peace and prosperity of Jerusalem. These little psalms all breathe a spirit of quiet, undaunted faith in Israel's God, *the Maker of heaven and earth* (Psalm 121:2; 124:7; 134:4).

¹I lift up my eyes to the hills –
  where does my help come from?
²My help comes from the LORD,
  the Maker of heaven and earth.

³He will not let your foot slip –
  he who watches over you will not
  slumber;

⁴indeed, he who watches over Israel
  will neither slumber nor sleep.

⁵The LORD watches over you –
  the LORD is your shade at your right
  hand;
⁶the sun will not harm you by day,
  nor the moon by night.

⁷The LORD will keep you from all harm –
  he will watch over your life;
⁸the LORD will watch over your coming
  and going
  both now and for evermore.

As they approached the hills surrounding Jerusalem, Psalm 121 would be an obviously suitable song for pilgrims to sing.

In the opening two verses the psalmist speaks in the first person singular, *I*. To his question in verse 1 about the source of his help comes his answer: *My help comes from the LORD, the Maker of heaven and earth* (verse 2). This sentence contains a remarkable combination of ideas, that Jehovah, the covenant God of Israel, is the creator of the universe. In verse 4 He is further described as the keeper of Israel, who neither slumbers nor sleeps. This, then, is the ground of the author's faith in God's ability to keep, namely the almighty power of the world's creator and the ceaseless vigilance of Israel's guardian.

Having talked to himself, the psalmist now addresses some fellow-pilgrim, and the rest of his song expresses variations on the theme of God's keeping power. Although our English translation conceals the fact by using the words *keep* and *watch over*, the same Hebrew word which they translate actually occurs six times (verses 3,4,5, twice in verse 7, verse 8). He who keeps the nation Israel is also the keeper of the individual Israelite (verses 4,5). He will keep him *from all harm,* watch over his *life* and his *coming and going... for evermore* (verses 7,8).

Opposite: The Dome of
the Rock from inside the
Dominus Flevit Chapel,
built to remind us that
when Jesus came to
Jerusalem for the last time
he wept over the city.

Psalm 122

The Peace of Jerusalem

This psalm is, more obviously than all the other "Songs of Ascents," a song for pilgrims going up to Jerusalem for one of the feasts.

The first verse expresses the thrill the psalmist felt when he was invited to join the pilgrimage. By verse 2 he and the other pilgrims have arrived at their destination. Different thoughts begin to crowd into his mind as he looks round about him. He notices how *closely compacted* the city is (verse 3). He also recalls God's purpose that the tribes should visit it for the yearly festivals *according to the statute given to Israel*, referring no doubt to the law recorded in Exodus 23:17. He remembers that Jerusalem is the centre of the nation's religious and political life, where the people may either praise the Lord or approach the *thrones for judgment*, if they have some dispute or law suit pending (verses 4,5).

After his meditation, the psalmist breaks out into a plea that people will pray for the peace of Jerusalem, and he gives them a prayer to use (verses 6,7). Having asked others to pray, he now prays himself. For the sake of his fellow-pilgrims and *for the sake of the house of the LORD our God* (which, above all, makes Jerusalem so precious), he will seek her *prosperity* (verses 8,9).

1 I rejoiced with those who said to me,
  "Let us go to the house of the LORD."
2 Our feet are standing
  in your gates, O Jerusalem.

3 Jerusalem is built like a city
  that is closely compacted together.
4 That is where the tribes go up,
  the tribes of the LORD,
to praise the name of the LORD
  according to the statue given to
    Israel.
5 There the thrones for judgment stand,
  the thrones of the house of David.

6 Pray for the peace of Jerusalem:
  "May those who love you be secure.
7 May there be peace within your walls
  and security within your citadels."
8 For the sake of my brothers and
    friends,
  I will say, "Peace be within you."
9 For the sake of the house of the LORD
    our God,
  I will seek your prosperity.

The snow-capped peak of Mount Hermon, in the far north of Israel.

Psalm 123

The Uplifted Eyes of Faith

The background of this psalm is the scornful opposition of the *proud* and the *arrogant* (verse 4). We can only guess to whom the author is referring. It may have been any of Israel's enemies. But it certainly fits Sanballat the Horonite, Tobiah the Ammonite, and Geshem the Arab, who, when they heard of the Jews' resolve to rebuild the city wall, derided and despised them (see Nehemiah 2:19; 4:1-5).

The opening verses give a beautiful picture of quiet, patient confidence in the God who is enthroned in heaven (verse 1). As the servant's eyes look to the hand of his master, and the maid's to her mistress's, *so our eyes look to the LORD our God* (verse 2). This eye-to-hand gaze, as the analogy demands, expresses a waiting not for instructions but for provisions. It symbolises dependence, not obedience.

Having declared that he is patiently waiting for God's mercy, the psalmist now prays for it. His prayer is not an individual one; he identifies himself with the nation: *we have endured much ridicule from the proud.*

---

[1] I lift up my eyes to you,
    to you whose throne is in heaven.
[2] As the eyes of slaves look to the hand
    of their master,
  as the eyes of a maid look to the
    hand of her mistress,
  so our eyes look to the LORD our God,
    till he shows us his mercy.

[3] Have mercy on us, O LORD, have
    mercy on us,
  for we have endured much
    contempt.
[4] We have endured much ridicule from
    the proud,
  much contempt from the arrogant.

Opposite: The Greek
Orthodox monastery
perched precariously on
the side of the Mount of
Temptation, near Jericho.
Tradition has it that here
Jesus was tempted by
Satan.

Psalm 125

The Mountains round Mount Zion

Most of Palestine is mountainous terrain, and mountains
played an important part in the history of Israel. The pilgrims
approaching Jerusalem naturally sang about them (see also
Psalm 121:1).

Two mountain metaphors are combined. First, believers are
like Mount Zion itself, standing firm. Secondly, they are like
Jerusalem encircled by mountains, for they are themselves surrounded by the protection of Jehovah. Thus, God's people are
like a mountain surrounded by mountains, both immovable
and impregnable (verses 1,2).

The metaphors are now applied. God will not allow *the
sceptre of the wicked* (verse 3), which may refer to the machi-
nations of the Persian-dominated Samaritans, to rule in the
land which He has *allotted to the righteous*, lest the righteous
use their hands to do evil. On the contrary, the psalmist prays
with confidence that God will *do good... to those who are
good*, but drive away the evildoers (verses 4,5).

¹Those who trust in the LORD are like
Mount Zion,
which cannot be shaken but
endures for ever.
²As the mountains surround Jerusalem.
so the LORD surrounds his people
both now and for evermore.

³The sceptre of the wicked will not
remain
over the land allotted to the
righteous,
for then the righteous might use
their hands to do evil.

⁴Do good, O LORD, to those who are
good,
to those who are upright in heart.
⁵But those who turn to crooked ways
the LORD will banish with the
evildoers.

Peace be upon Israel.

An orthodox rabbi leads a group of young Jewish children across the Temple square in front of the Western Wall, Jerusalem

Psalm 127

The Vanity of Unblessed Labor

It is useless to launch a new enterprise or attempt to guard an old one, unless the Lord blesses these labors (verse 1). The house builder's labor is vain unless the Lord does the building, and the city watchman's vigilance is vain unless the Lord does the watching. We may toil and overwork, getting up early and going to bed late, but all the time, if we only knew it, God grants *sleep to those he loves* (verse 2) or "gives to his beloved in sleep" (Revised Standard Version). This, of course, is not a condemnation of industry, any more than our Lord's teaching in Matthew 6:25-34 is a prohibition of prudent forethought. What is condemned is worry on the one hand, and feverish self-confident activity on the other. Both are symptoms of unbelief.

Children must be recognised as *a heritage from the* L ORD (verse 3), one of God's most precious gifts. *Sons born in one's youth are like arrows* (verse 4), for by the time their warrior father is aged they themselves will be old enough to defend and protect him. Moreover, if his *quiver is full of them,* he will be able to hold his own in any disputes *in the gate,* that is, in the space near the city gate where business is transacted and lawsuits are heard.

¹Unless the L ORD builds the house,
   its builders labour in vain.
Unless the L ORD watches over the
   city,
   the watchmen stand guard in vain.
²In vain you rise early
   and stay up late,
toiling for food to eat –
   for he grants sleep to those he
    loves.

³Sons are a heritage from the L ORD,
   children a reward from him.
⁴Like arrows in the hands of a warrior
   are sons born in one's youth.
⁵Blessed is the man
   whose quiver is full of them.
They will not be put to shame
   when they contend with their
    enemies in the gate.

Opposite: A stone-built watchtower in fields in the West Bank, near Samaria. Farmers slept in such watchtowers during harvest to guard their crops from thieves.

Psalm 130

Out of the Depths

The author's experience of forgiveness leads him to urge Israel to trust God for redemption.

The psalmist depicts himself as floundering in deep waters, and *out of the depths* he appeals to God to rescue him (verses 1,2). These deep waters are a picture of his sin, guilt, and sense of God's judgment – his own, and perhaps the nation's too, with which he identifies himself (compare Nehemiah 1:4-7). The author knows that if God *kept a record of sins*, taking them into account and reckoning them up against him, neither he nor anyone else *could stand* (verse 3). *But with you*, he immediately adds, *there is forgiveness* (verse 4).

It was this offer of forgiveness by grace without works, which led Luther to call this penitential song one of the "Pauline Psalms". Verse 4 was also one of the Scripture verses which brought comfort to John Bunyan, author of *Pilgrim's Progress*, when he was convicted of sin. It contains a beautiful balance, because its first part brings assurance to the despairing, while its second part sounds a warning to the presumptuous. Far from encouraging sinners in their sins, God's forgiveness promotes that fear of the Lord, or reverent awe in His presence, which leads men and women to depart from iniquity (compare Proverbs 16:6).

Confident of the forgiving mercy of God to sinners, the author now does two things. First, he affirms his own determination to trust God for it. The ground of his faith is God's promise (verse 5). Thus assured, his soul *waits for the LORD* (verse 6). His guilty conscience has brought him into the darkness, but he longs and waits expectantly for the dawn of God's pardoning grace. Secondly, he urges Israel to do the same. His conviction regarding his own forgiveness (verse 4) leads him to affirm that *with the LORD is unfailing love* for Israel's sin as well (verse 7).

¹Out of the depths I cry to you, O LORD;
² O Lord, hear my voice.
Let your ears be attentive
to my cry for mercy.

³If you, O LORD, kept a record of sins,
O Lord, who could stand?
⁴But with you there is forgiveness;
therefore you are feared.

⁵I wait for the LORD, my soul waits,
and in his word I put my hope.
⁶My soul waits for the Lord
more than watchmen wait for the morning,
more than watchmen wait for the morning.

⁷O Israel, put your hope in the LORD,
for with the LORD is unfailing love
and with him is full redemption.
⁸He himself will redeem Israel
from all their sins.

A young Arab boy in
Bethlehem. This psalm
portrays the child-like
humility which God
demands of us.

Psalm 131

A Child-like Humility

These words, which paint the picture of a little child's contented dependence on its mother, seem to anticipate our Lord's insistence on the necessity of a child-like humility.

The psalmist contrasts what he is not with what he is. He is not haughty, he says, in either heart or looks. He does not occupy himself with *great matters* (verse 1). That is, he has renounced proud ambitions for prestige and power, whether for himself personally or for Israel after the Restoration, still humiliated under a foreign yoke. Instead, he is willing to be like a *weaned child*, no longer crying to be suckled, yet nestling contentedly at its mother's breast (verse 2). The condition thus pictorially described seems to be a person (or nation) who, weaned from arrogant ambitions, finds perfect satisfaction in God. It is a beautiful picture not only of humble faith but of what might be called the "motherhood" of God.

As in Psalm 130, the psalmist leaves his description of the lesson he has learned and urges Israel to learn it too. *O Israel, put your hope in the LORD both now and evermore* (verse 3).

¹My heart is not proud, O LORD,
 my eyes are not haughty;
I do not concern myself with great
  matters
 or things too wonderful for me.
²But I have stilled and quieted my soul;
 like a weaned child with its mother,
 like a weaned child is my soul within
  me.

³O Israel, put your hope in the LORD
 both now and for evermore.

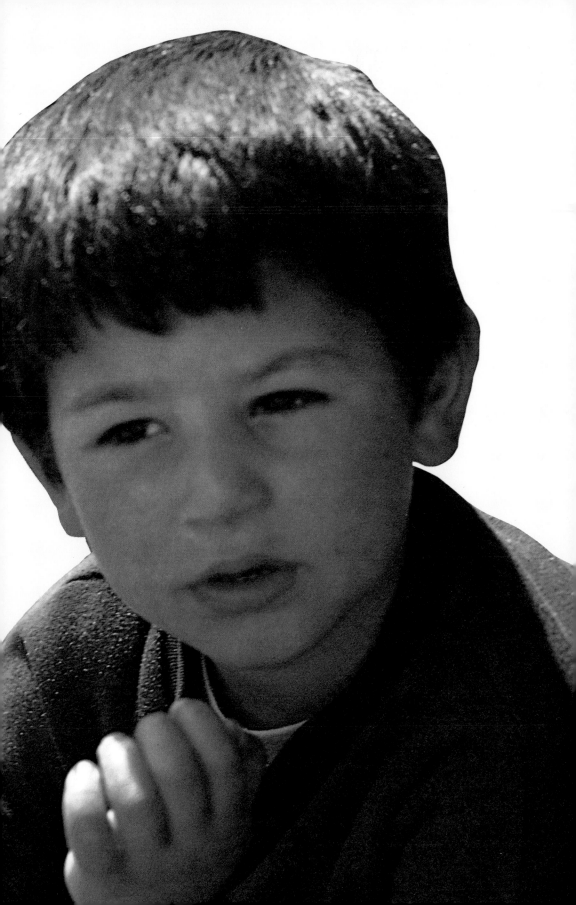

Opposite: An old Jewish
man studies the Scriptures
in the shadow of the
Western Wall, Jerusalem.

Psalm 133

Brothers Dwelling in Unity

The unity of the people of God has always been both His will
and the object of their desire. If this psalm is post-Exilic, it may
express the joy and solidarity of pilgrims gathered for worship
in Jerusalem, with the breach of the divided monarchy healed.

The covenant people of God are already *brothers*; but it is
both *good and pleasant* if, in addition to their fraternal
relationship, they *live together in unity* (verse 1). The pleasant-
ness of unity is now vividly illustrated. It is like the consecrating oil *running down on Aaron's beard* (from his head on
which it had been poured) and flowing down on to the *collar
of his robes*, and like *the dew of Hermon*, an expression for
heavy dew (verses 2,3).

We are not told why the unity of the people of God is like
Aaron's consecrating oil and Hermon's heavy dew. Some writers have emphasised that both are said to descend, and that
their significance is the all-embracing influence of true
brotherly concord, sanctifying the whole body. At the same
time, since aromatic oil will have been used and the dew was
essential to the fertility of arid Palestine, these similes are
surely meant also to teach that unity is as fragrant as oil and as
refreshing as dew in Jerusalem. It is there that Jehovah *bestows
blessing, even life for evermore* (verse 3).

> ¹How good and pleasant it is
>   when brothers live together in unity!
> ²It is like precious oil poured on the
>   head,
>   running down on the beard,
>   running down on Aaron's beard,
>   down upon the collar of his robes.
> ³It is as if the dew of Hermon
>   were falling on Mount Zion.
> For there the LORD bestows his
>   blessing,
>   even life for evermore.

Sunset over the Sea of Galilee. "Even the darkness will not be dark to you; the night will shine like the day, for the darkness is as light to you."

Psalm 139

The All-seeing Eye of God

This has been called "the crown of all psalms." It is certainly a sublime exposition of one man's personal awareness of God's universal knowledge and presence. It is best known for verses 6 to 11, which unfold the impossibility of escape from God.

God's omniscience (verses 1-6)

The verbs paint a picture of God's perfect knowledge of humankind. He "searches," "knows," "perceives," "discerns," and is "familiar with" everything about us (verses 1-3). The divine knowledge extends to our thoughts, deeds, and words. First, God knows our thoughts *from afar* (verse 2). "Neither space nor time exist for God" (Bishop Perowne); all human thoughts are open before Him. Next, God perceives *all my ways*, including the activities of the day and the rest of the night (verses 2,3). Thirdly, God knows the words of our tongue, even before they are spoken (verse 4).

¹O LORD, you have searched me
  and you know me.
²You know when I sit and when I rise;
  you perceive my thoughts from afar.
³You discern my going out and my lying
    down;
  you are familiar with all my ways.
⁴Before a word is on my tongue
  you know it completely, O LORD.

⁵You hem me in, behind and before;
  you have laid your hand upon me.
⁶Such knowledge is too wonderful for
    me,
  too lofty for me to attain.

⁷Where can I go from your Spirit?
  Where can I flee from your
    presence?
⁸If I go up to the heavens, you are there;
  if I make my bed in the depths, you
    are there.
⁹If I rise on the wings of the dawn,
  if I settle on the far side of the sea,
¹⁰even there your hand will guide me,
  your right hand will hold me fast.

¹¹If I say, "Surely the darkness will hide
    me
  and the light become night around
    me,"
¹²even the darkness will not be dark to
    you;
  the night will shine like the day,
  for the darkness is as light to you.

¹³For you created my inmost being;
  you knit me together in my mother's
    womb.
¹⁴I praise you because I am fearfully and
    wonderfully made;
  your works are wonderful,
  I know that full well.
¹⁵My frame was not hidden from you
  when I was made in the secret place.
  When I was woven together in the
    depths of the earth,
¹⁶ your eyes say my unformed body.
  All the days ordained for me
  were written in your book
  before one of them came to be.

¹⁷How precious to me are your thoughts,
    O God!
  How vast is the sum of them!
¹⁸Were I to count them,
  they would outnumber the grains of
    sand.
  When I awake
  I am still with you.

¹⁹If only you would slay the wicked, O
    God!
  Away from me, you bloodthirsty
    men!
²⁰They speak of you with evil intent;
  your adversaries misuse your name.
²¹Do I not hate those who hate you, O
    LORD,
  and abhor those who rise up against
    you?
²²I have nothing but hatred for them;
  I count them my enemies.

²³Search me, O God, and know my heart;
  test me and know my anxious
    thoughts.
²⁴See if there is any offensive way in me,
  and lead me in the way everlasting.

In verse 5, the psalmist begins to anticipate the theme of the next paragraph and attributes God's knowledge of him to His constant presence both *behind and before*. He pictures himself as a beleaguered city. But this encompassing presence of God fills him with wonder, not fear, and he breaks out in praise of God's amazing, unattainable knowledge (verse 6).

God's omnipresence (verses 7-12)

This section begins with a question: *Where can I go from your Spirit?* (verse 7). It is important to observe, however, that this question expresses not the desire to escape, but the joyful astonishment that escape is impossible and that God's hand is everywhere to guide and hold him (verse 10). In order to emphasise the impossibility of escape from God, he mentions three conceivable escape routes or hiding places and declares that even there God is present. Thus, if he should ascend to heaven or descend to Sheol, the abode of the dead, God is there (verse 8). If he should *rise on the wings of the dawn*, a beautiful figure of speech for traveling at the speed of light, and reach *the far side of the sea*, even there too he would find God. No distance, from farthest east to farthest west, can separate him from God (verses (9,10). Next, if he should try to hide from God in the darkness, he would discover that God's eyes pierce through the gloom, since to God *darkness is as light* (verses 11,12).

God's omnipotence (verses 13-18)

God's omniscience, which in the previous section has been attributed to his omnipresence, is now attributed to His omnipotence. God can search man out not only because He sees him, but because He made him. The Creator knows His creatures through and through. The psalmist ascribes the wonderful development of the embryo in the womb to the creative power of God. Both his *inmost being* and his *frame* (verses 13,15) are God's. These together comprehend human beings, our body and our mind, emotions and will. The phrase *fearfully and wonderfully made* (verse 14), was originally suggested by the translator Miles Coverdale, but may be incorrect. Other modern translations render the phrase "for thou art fearful and wonderful." This wonderful creator-God, while fashioning the writer, naturally saw his *unformed body* (verse 16). More than that, even before he was born, all the days of his life were planned and recorded in God's book (verses 15,16). Such divine knowledge and foreknowledge cause the psalmist to burst into praise. For the thoughts of God, which he calls *precious and vast*, outnumber *the grains of sand* (verses 17,18).

He ends the paragraph with a statement whose meaning is

doubtful: *When I awake, I am still with you* (verse 18). Some writers suppose that he is referring again, as in the first two verses, to God's continuous presence with him whether he wakes or sleeps. Others think that he is referring to awaking from the sleep of death.

God's judgment (verses 19-24)

If only you would slay the wicked, O God! (verse 19). Many Christian readers feel that this sudden prayer sounds a jarring note after what has gone before. Yet it is perfectly consistent with it. When a person's world is full of God, they long for the elimination of evil. These evildoers are described both as *bloodthirsty* (verse 19) and as those who misuse God's name (verse 20), either taking His name in vain or exalting themselves against His authority. That is, they set themselves against both God and their fellows. In utter revolt against God's two great commandments to love Him and their neighbor, they do not even stop short of blood (violence, murder) or of blasphemy.

This, then, is the first point to notice. The psalmist is not expressing feelings of personal animosity or revenge. He has come to count God's enemies (verse 20) as his own enemies (verse 22). He is righteously indignant, where we would be unrighteously tolerant. He burns with a divine hatred of sin.

But, it may be said, this man failed to distinguish between evil and the evildoer. Should he (and we with him) not learn to love the sinner and hate the sin? Of course there is some truth in this. Yet it can be overpressed, for "evil" is not something abstract; it exists in the hearts and ways of evildoers. So when the judgment of God falls, it will fall upon evildoers, not upon evil in the abstract.

But, an objector may further ask, while hope remains we should surely desire not judgment of sinners, but their salvation? Yes indeed, but what if sinners refuse to repent? We cannot desire their salvation in defiance of their own willingness to receive it. This is the heart of the matter. The Bible teaches that the sinner is at one and the same time the object of God's love and wrath (compare John 3:16,36), and we should seek by grace at least to approximate our attitude to God's. We should earnestly desire the salvation of sinners if they will repent, and equally earnestly their (and indeed our own) destruction if they (or we) will not. It is because we find it difficult if not impossible to feel such sentiments, in divine purity without any admixture of personal venom, that we cannot easily echo the psalmist's words. But let us acknowledge the reason: it is because we know little of a truly righteous indignation .

Opposite: A woman guides a blind man through the narrow streets of the old city of Jerusalem. "The LORD is gracious and compassionate, slow to anger and rich in love."

Psalm 145

In Praise of God's Kingdom

The "kingdom" of God is the rule of God, both generally over the universe and particularly over His people, and it is this that is celebrated in Psalm 145. It is an acrostic psalm, each verse beginning with a different letter of the Hebrew alphabet in sequence, but its one theme is the glory and graciousness of Jehovah's rule. The praise which He deserves from His citizens is eternal and rational.

Eternal praise (verses 1-7)
The psalm opens with the author's resolve to exalt and praise God not only *every day* (verse 2) but *for ever and ever* (verses 1,2). Because the Lord is great, He is *most worthy of praise* (verse 3); since *no-one can fathom* His greatness, His praise must be unceasing. But no individual can worship God for ever on earth. So the author seems to be speaking as the representative of Israel and to be referring to future generations, each of which will declare God's work to the next and so perpetuate His praise (verse 4). They will be occupied with *your wonderful works, your awesome works, your great deeds* (verses 5-7).

¹I will exalt you, my God the King;
  I will praise your name for ever and
    ever.
²Every day I will praise you
  and extol your name for ever and
    ever.

³Great is the LORD and most worthy of
    praise;
  his greatness no-one can fathom.
⁴One generation will commend your
    works to another;
  they will tell of your mighty acts.
⁵They will speak of the glorious
    splendour of your majesty,
  and I will meditate on your wonderful
    works.
⁶They will tell of the power of your
    awesome works,
  and I will proclaim your great deeds.
⁷They will celebrate your abundant
    goodness
  and joyfully sing of your
    righteousness.

⁸The LORD is gracious and
    compassionate,
  slow to anger and rich in love.
⁹The LORD is good to all;
  he has compassion on all he has
    made.
¹⁰All you have made will praise you, O
    LORD;
  your saints will extol you.
¹¹They will tell of the glory of your
    kingdom
  and speak of your might,
¹²so that all men may know of your
    mighty acts
  and the glorious splendour of your
    kingdom.
¹³Your kingdom is an everlasting
    kingdom,
  and your dominion endures through
    all generations.

The LORD is faithful to all his promises
  and loving towards all he has made.

¹⁴The LORD upholds all those who fall
  and lifts up all who are bowed down.
¹⁵The eyes of all look to you,
  and give them their food at the
    proper time.
¹⁶You open your hand
  and satisfy the desires of every living
    thing.

¹⁷The LORD is righteous in all his ways
  and loving towards all he has made.
¹⁸The LORD is near to all who call on him,
  to all who call on him in truth.
¹⁹He fulfils the desires of those who fear
    him;
  he hears their cry and saves them.
²⁰The LORD watches over all who love
    him,
  but all the wicked he will destroy.
²¹My mouth will speak in praise of the
    LORD.
  Let every creature praise his holy
    name for ever and ever.

Universal praise (verses 8-13)

The praise which is due to God is also universal, offered to Him by all His creatures. This is only logical, because *he has compassion on all he has made* (verse 9). The glory that is given by human beings to God is a response to the grace that is given to them by God. And God gives grace because He is gracious. Ultimately, both the eternity and the universality of worship arise from the gracious character of God. Verse 8 echoes Jehovah's self-revelation to Moses recorded in Exodus 34:6 and already quoted in Psalm 103:8. His nature of grace and mercy expresses itself in universal goodness to humankind (verse 9). Hence the universality of His praise. Human beings sing the glory, the power, and the eternity of His kingdom (verses 11-13). The words anticipate the doxology at the end of the Lord's Prayer: "Yours is the kingdom and the power and the glory for ever. Amen" (Matthew 6:13).

Rational praise (verses 14-21)

The praise which is to ascend to God for all time and from all people is intelligent worship, or what the Lord Jesus called "worship... in truth" (John 4:24). The only worship which is acceptable to God is offered in rational response to His revelation of Himself. That is, it is a worship of His *name* (verses 1,2,21), His eternal being as made known in His words and works.

The psalmist now gives some concrete examples of God's gracious works. They show that His rule, though powerful, is not arbitrary. On the contrary, His kingdom is a beneficent kingdom, and His throne a throne of grace. See how He condescends to succour His people in all their need. He upholds the falling and raises the fallen (verse 14). He feeds the hungry and satisfies *the desires of every living thing* (verses 15,16). He comes close to those who call upon Him; He hears and answers their prayers (verses 18,19). He protects those who love Him, but *will destroy* the wicked (verse 20).

It is noteworthy that in verses 19 and 20 God's people are said both to *fear* and to *love* Him. One writer comments: "Fear and love are the inseparable elements of true religion. Fear preserves love from degenerating into presumptuous familiarity: love prevents fear from becoming a servile and cringing dread."

The last verse (verse 21) seems to summarise the three characteristics of the worship of Jehovah, which have been elaborated in the psalm. It is eternal (*for ever and ever*), universal (*every creature*), and rational (*praise his holy name*).

Psalm 150

The Final Doxology

The Psalter's doxology forms a fitting conclusion. As a summons to worship it is unsurpassed in grandeur. In common with the Hallel (Psalms 113-118) and the four preceding psalms (146-149), it begins and ends with the word Hallelujah or *Praise the LORD*. Further, every verse is an invitation to praise, telling us where and why, how and by whom, the praise of God should be expressed.

Where and why (verses 1,2)
Praise God in his sanctuary. The catalogue of musical instruments which follows clearly relates to Temple worship. But God is to be praised *in his mighty heavens* too (verse 1). So probably this verse is an invitation to both humans and angels to worship God — humans in earth's sanctuary, and angels in heaven. It reminds us that the praise of God is one, the church below joining "angels and archangels and all the company of heaven" in His worship.

The reasons why God is to be praised are found in His works and His nature, His doing and His being (verse 2). His *acts of power* are not specified, but will include His works of creation, preservation, providence, and redemption. They are the expression of His *surpassing greatness*. This is the perennial theme of worship — the greatness of God displayed in His works.

¹Praise the LORD.

Praise God in his sanctuary;
　　praise him in his mighty heavens.
²Praise him for his acts of power;
　　praise him for his surpassing
　　　greatness.
³Praise him with the sounding of the
　　　trumpet,
　　praise him with the harp and lyre,
⁴praise him with tambourine and
　　　dancing,
　　praise him with the strings and flute,
⁵praise him with the clash of cymbals,
　　praise him with resounding cymbals.

⁶Let everything that has breath praise
　　　the LORD.

Praise the LORD.

Opposite: A Jewish
religious leader blows the
shofar, the ancient ram's
horn trumpet, used in
ancient Israel to summon
the people on military and
religious occasions.

How and by whom (verses 3-6)

Every conceivable instrument is to be employed in the worship of Jehovah: wind, strings, and percussion (compare Psalm 81:1-3). The first is *the trumpet*, the ancient curved ram's horn. This is "the only musical instrument still in use in the synagogue", writes one commentator, "and the expert can make a prodigious noise with it." The other two instruments mentioned in verse 3 are stringed, *the harp and lyre*. Next come the *tambourine and dancing* (verse 4), and then *the strings and flute*, the latter being perhaps the simple shepherd's pipe. Verse 5 mentions two cymbals; the first possibly as small as castanets, the second larger and thus *resounding*.

So the orchestra is assembled. Worshipers are to blow the horn and pluck the harp, beat the drum, sweep the strings, play the flute, and clang the cymbals. "Noise, you may well say. Mere music is not enough... Let us have clashing cymbals, not only well tuned, but *loud*, and dances too," writes C.S.Lewis. What is here described is the uninhibited exuberance of lives devoted to God.

Nevertheless, the mere noise of instruments and movements of dancing are not acceptable to God, however beautiful, unless they express the devotion of our hearts and minds . The psalm's concluding verse (6), which calls on *everything that has breath* to praise God, may be intended to include the animal creation. Yet the emphasis is upon us human beings, the crown of God's creation, into whom He breathed the breath of life (Genesis 2:7). Our worship is not to be confined to church services. On the contrary, while we breathe, we praise.